FINANCING AND RISK IN
DEVELOPING COUNTRIES

Based on the
Proceedings of a Symposium
on Developing Countries' Debt
Sponsored by the Export-Import
Bank of the United States
in April 1977

FINANCING AND RISK IN DEVELOPING COUNTRIES

edited by
Stephen H. Goodman

PRAEGER PUBLISHERS
Praeger Special Studies

New York　　•　　London　　•　　Sydney　　•　　Toronto

51612

Views expressed herein must be considered the views of the individual authors. They do not purport to promulgate or voice the views of the Export-Import Bank of the United States, nor any other agency of the United States.

PRAEGER PUBLISHERS
PRAEGER SPECIAL STUDIES
383 Madison Avenue, New York, N.Y. 10017, U.S.A.

Published in the United States of America in 1978
by Praeger Publishers,
A Division of Holt, Rinehart and Winston, CBS, Inc.

89   038   987654321

Library of Congress Catalog Card Number: 78-63013

Printed in the United States of America

Stephen H. Goodman
Robert Z. Aliber
Anthony G. Barrett
David O. Beim
Jerome K. Blask
A. Bruce Brackenridge
William R. Cline
Stephen M. Dubrul, Jr.
Stephen D. Eccles
Richard D. Erb
Irving S. Friedman

John A. Holsen
Charles P. Kindleberger
Lawrence B. Krause
Alice L. Mayo
Jo W. Saxe
Roman Senkiw
Robert L. Slighton
Anthony M. Solomon
James B. Thornblade
Henry C. Wallich

CONTENTS

LIST OF TABLES

INTRODUCTION: AN OVERVIEW
OF FINANCING AND RISK
IN DEVELOPING COUNTRIES
Stephen H. Goodman

This volume and the conference for which the chapters were prepared reflect the importance that Eximbank and other serious international lenders attach to understanding and managing the risks associated with foreign lending. While thoughtful lenders have always recognized the importance of understanding and managing risk, this task has been given added impetus by the massive increase in lending—particularly to developing countries—and by increased economic uncertainty in the world. Reflecting these trends, growing attention is now being paid to the issue of financing and risk in developing countries, not only by lenders, but also by bank regulators, politicians, security analysts, journalists, and the public at large.

At the end of 1977 the disbursed debt outstanding of the non-OPEC* developing countries (not including Greece, Israel, Portugal, Spain, and Turkey) total led about $180 billion—an almost threefold increase since 1971. Of this total, about $80 billion will represent developing-country debt to banks and other private financial institutions. In the largest U.S. banks, the share of developing-country credits in the total portfolio now ranges as high as 30 percent and is still growing. Because of this massive increase in developing-country debt and the growing role of private lenders, the question is increasingly being asked: Can the developing countries service and repay their debt, and, if they can't, what are the consequences for private banks, the international financial system, and international economic relations?

We hope this volume will provide at least a tentative answer to this question and also will suggest new approaches to international exposure and risk management, including a number of techniques for assessing country risk.

NATURE OF THE PROBLEM

A first step toward understanding the problem of financing and risk in developing countries is to recognize that one cannot deal in simple aggregates. There are very different types of risk depending both on the nature of the transaction and the particular country. The risks are quite different, for example, in providing short-term trade financing, in extending a term loan for balance-of-payments purposes, or in operating a branch network borrowing and lending in foreign currencies (the latter is frequently not considered a foreign risk). Simi-

---

*Organization of Petroleum Exporting Countries.

larly, the risks are quite different in lending to Iran rather than to Brazil, or to Argentina, Zaire, or Bangladesh.

Private-bank lending is concentrated—possibly as much as 80 percent—in lower-risk transactions, principally those with maturities of less than one year and often guaranteed by the government or a multinational corporation in a developed country. The poorest developing countries hold very little of the private-bank debt—basically because few banks would lend to them.

One can distinguish between the aid developing countries, whose foreign exchange needs can be satisfied through grants or very soft loans, and the commercial developing countries, who have regular access to, and rely on, commercial financing to cover their exchange requirements. Two commercial countries—Brazil and Mexico—probably account for roughly one-third of the developing countries' total disbursed debt outstanding; ten additional countries—Argentina, Chile, Colombia, Peru, the Philippines, South Korea, Taiwan, Thailand, Turkey, and Zaire—account for about one-half of the remainder. Most of these countries are in the upper tier of the developing countries in terms of level of development and income. The principal focus of this volume is on financing and risk in these countries.

ROOTS OF THE PROBLEM

The commercial developing countries' ability and willingness to tap external resources and put them to productive use in the development process resulted both in a massive increase in developing-country indebtedness and cushioned the economic adjustment following the sharp rise in oil prices and the world recession in 1974/75. Rather than drastically cutting import volume with immediate detrimental effects on both economic development and domestic welfare, the commercial developing countries chose to pursue fairly consistent economic policies while borrowing to finance growing payments deficits.

As a consequence of this policy, the non-OPEC developing countries as a group ran large current account deficits in 1974 and 1975 (about $28 billion and $34 billion, respectively, before official transfers, compared with deficits of $6 to $8 billion annually in the previous decade). Although the non-OPEC developing countries did remarkably well during 1976, substantially reducing their payments deficit (to around $25 billion), they nevertheless still borrowed heavily to balance their external accounts and to boost their international reserves, increasing their total disbursed debt outstanding to about $160 billion at year-end.

The massive size and rapid and continuing growth in developing country debt account for much of the concern about financing and risk in developing countries and serve as important backdrops to the chapters in this volume.

BENEFITS OF INFLATION

Although the absolute size and rate of growth of developing-country debt are unprecedented, it is important to note that, to a large extent, they merely reflect the worldwide inflation of the last several years—an inflation that has benefited the developing countries, as it has most debtors.

The prices of developing-country exports have more than doubled since 1971; indeed, in a single year—1974—export prices rose a startling 44 percent. Because of this rapid rise in prices, there has been a substantial reduction in the real value of the developing countries' debt-service burden from what would otherwise have been the case. In the 1971-76 period, the debt relief provided through inflation averaged $13 billion annually, more than twice the average annual flow of grants during the period.

In real terms, the disbursed debt outstanding of the developing countries is only about 15 percent greater today than it was in 1971 compared with about a 150 percent increase in the nominal value of the developing countries' debt during the period. Moreover, the ratio of developing-country exports to debt—and consequently the developing countries' ability to service their debt—is actually significantly greater today (.77 to 1) than it was in 1971 (.66 to 1), reflecting both the rapid growth in developing-country export prices and the substantial growth in developing-country export volume.

The international reserves of the developing countries have also increased dramatically, growing from $11 billion in 1971 to over $40 billion today. Adjusting the data on disbursed debt outstanding to reflect this increase, the increase in other developing-country assets, and the reduction of other developing-country liabilities results in an even more dramatic improvement in the ratio of developing-country exports to debt.

SERVICING THEIR DEBT

Although developing-country debt is likely to continue to grow for the foreseeable future, it is important to recognize that, to a large extent, this merely reflects a more efficient worldwide allocation of capital.

Clearly, the non-OPEC developing countries will be unable to repay their debt anytime soon, but this is equally true of the U.S. government and General Motors, to cite two examples. The issue is not whether the developing countries will be able to repay their debt, but rather whether they will continue to be able to service their debt—that is, to pay interest—and to roll over the principal on their existing debt and arrange additional financing.

If the developing countries are to continue servicing their debt without reducing their standard of living, they must channel their borrowing, directly or indirectly, into productive investment. This investment, if properly managed, will generate the additional goods and services, and exports, needed to pay the interest and other financing charges.

Since World War II, most developing countries have channeled their borrowings into productive investment. This is reflected in the relatively few cases of default or rescheduling during the period. Moreover, the relatively few default or rescheduling episodes that have occurred have generally followed periods in which borrowed resources were diverted to consumption, both personal and national.

Given the existing worldwide distribution of capital, labor, and resources, the productivity of capital is probably higher today in the developing countries than in the developed countries. An efficient allocation of capital would consequently suggest more lending to developing countries, not less. The more mature economies such as the United States should be net capital exporters while the developing countries should be net capital importers.

Many developing countries, however, may face difficulties in raising the additional capital that they need, and which they can effectively use and can afford. The developing countries will have to borrow about $25 billion in each of the next several years if they are to realize their growth potential; if they continue to rely as heavily on private banks as they have since 1973, their indebtedness to banks and other private lenders will have to increase between $10 and $15 billion annually. While such an increase is not inconceivable, it will be difficult, due to the projected growth of loan demand in industrial countries and growing concern over the relatively high proportion of developing-country credits in commercial bank loan portfolios. Difficulties may become particularly pronounced in 1978 when loan demand in industrial countries is expected to recover and the developing countries will begin rolling over the credits extended at the beginning of the oil crisis.

As things stand now, the developing countries probably will be unable to obtain the financing necessary to achieve the rates of growth to which they were accustomed in the 1960s and early 1970s—and the rates of growth that they could achieve if adequate financing were available. The policy response of governments and the attitude of private lenders in industrial countries will be important factors in helping to determine the severity of the financial squeeze on developing-country growth. The chapters presented here, at least in a small way, should help assure that the policy response and the attitudes are the rights ones.

OUTLINE OF BOOK

The four principal sections of the book deal with the role of private lending in the developing countries, the debt situation of the developing countries and future prospects, international exposure and risk management, and techniques for assessing country risk.

Charles P. Kindleberger's chapter relates the present situation to episodes of international lending in the past. We have all heard the refrain that sovereign lending, even to developing countries, is essentially sound because countries don't disappear; while a commercial firm may go bankrupt, a country will only reschedule its obligations. This has by and large been true in the period since World War II. Kindleberger's chapter takes a somewhat longer view, however.

The chapters by Henry C. Wallich and Irving S. Friedman present two somewhat different views, from different vantage points, of the role of private bank lending in the developing countries. Wallich, speaking as a central banker, highlights some of the risks, and opportunities, in the current situation. Friedman, speaking as a private banker, emphasizes the role that private banks have played, and can continue to play, in the development process.

The chapters by Anthony M. Solomon, Jo W. Saxe, and Lawrence B. Krause attempt to reduce the confusion and uncertainty about the developing countries' current debt situation and future prospects. Treasury Undersecretary Solomon examines the developing-country debt problem in the broader perspective of the North/South dialogue and international monetary arrangements. Saxe explores some of the pitfalls in analyzing the nature and size of developing-country debt, particularly the dangers of looking at simple aggregates. Krause's contribution examines the outlook for the OPEC payments surplus, recognizing that the balance of payments of the OPEC countries impacts very directly on the payments prospects of the developing as well as the industrial countries.

The chapters by Stephen M. DuBrul, Jr., A. Bruce Brackenridge, and Jerome K. Blask describe various ways international lenders have sought to manage their foreign exposure and risk. DuBrul discusses some of the management procedures and techniques he recently introduced at Eximbank in this area, emphasizing the importance of integrating country risk analysis into an institution's overall planning. Brackenridge describes one approach, used by Morgan Guaranty Trust Company, to manage international exposure and assess country risk. Blask presents the results of a survey of 37 U.S. banks on their approaches and methodologies in evaluating country risk.

The contributions by James B. Thornblade, Alice L. Mayo and Anthony G. Barrett, and John A. Holsen examine three new techniques now being used to assess country risk. A checklist system, in which each country is rated with respect to various common indicators or variables and a composite score is calculated, is presented by Thornblade as a first step in assessing country risk. Mayo and Barrett describe a system which has had good results in distinguishing between those countries which may encounter repayment difficulties within the next five years and those which are unlikely to experience repayment difficulties. Holsen's contribution describes the elaborate and varied techniques the World Bank now uses in assessing country credit risk.

CONCLUSIONS

A number of common themes seem to emerge from these chapters, although the authors would not necessarily support each conclusion. The principal themes are these: despite continuing uncertainty, the repayment outlook on loans to the developing countries is generally good; private banks will, and should, continue to be an important source of financing for the developing countries; the present international payments situation, while posing a number of problems, also presents a unique opportunity to increase the level of global investment and economic growth; international exposure and risk management is extremely complex, but of increasing importance; and substantial progress is being made in developing better techniques for assessing country credit risk.

Many of the contributions reveal a sense of optimism regarding the repayment outlook for the developing countries. The new optimism is largely due both to the developing countries' strong economic performance during 1976, including their demonstrated willingness to adjust their economic policies—including slowing economic growth—when required to balance their external accounts, and to the growing recognition that the worldwide inflation during the last several years has substantially benefited the developing countries and that the current real payments deficit and outstanding debt of the developing countries are about what a projection of their historical trends would indicate.

Many of the contributions stress that private lenders should, and will, continue to be an important source of financing for the developing countries in the foreseeable future, but that private lenders must also continue to be selective and prudent. While some increase in the relative share of official lending in total lending was thought desirable, private lenders and markets were expected to carry the major financing burden. To facilitate this process, Henry Wallich suggests a modification in bank examination procedures to downplay the concept of "good" and "bad" loans and to emphasize instead proper portfolio management, including avoiding undue concentration in higher risk credits.

How well the developing countries, and the world economy, will fare will depend on many factors, especially the size of the OPEC payments surplus. While the OPEC surplus presents the rest of the world with a number of problems, it also presents, in the eyes of several of the authors, a unique opportunity to increase the level of global investment and economic growth. By discouraging consumption in industrial as well as developing countries, the OPEC surplus releases resources which are not currently needed in the OPEC countries and can consequently be channeled to increase worldwide investment, especially in developing countries where the productivity of capital is particularly high.

International exposure and risk management is of increasing importance, a number of the contributions note, reflecting the growth in developing-country debt and increased world economic uncertainty. There is a pressing need both for increased economic and financial information from the developing countries and improved risk management techniques if both public- and private-sector decision makers are to formulate reasonably accurate assessments of developing-country risk. National income, balance-of-payments, external debt, and debt-servicing data are needed on a timely and consistent basis.

Substantial progress is being made, many of the contributions suggest, in the ongoing efforts of public institutions and commercial banks to develop or refine better qualitative and quantitative techniques for assessing country risk. While most medium- and large-size banks have developed methods to assess country creditworthiness systematically, many are still dissatisfied with their existing evaluation procedures and are actively seeking new and better ones. Several contributors report on the procedures and techniques used in their institutions to assess country risk. The techniques range from the relatively qualitative country evaluation approach used at Morgan Guaranty to the more rigorous approach developed by Eximbank for identifying countries more likely to encounter repayment difficulties.

ROLE OF PRIVATE BANK LENDING
IN THE DEVELOPING COUNTRIES

DEBT SITUATION OF THE DEVELOPING COUNTRIES IN HISTORICAL PERSPECTIVE

Charles P. Kindleberger

It is impossible to present in a few pages a definitive treatise on the history of foreign borrowing by developing countries, and I will not attempt to do so. Instead, I will present an analytical account of such borrowing from the Napoleonic Wars to the eve of World War II, focusing primarily on the question of lending, the use of funds, and the burden of debt. My comments will not be statistical, nor will they be concerned with the problems of treating default— sending in the Marines, taking over customs duties, imposing capitulations, or organizing councils of foreign bondholders.

TYPES OF FOREIGN LENDING

I will discuss two types of foreign lending. One I call "boom lending" and the other I call "recycling lending." My discussion is an outgrowth of my research on what I call manias, panics, bubbles, crashes, and the role of the lender of last resort. My preoccupation has taken me back to the South Sea Bubble and John Law's Mississippi Bubble, and how far it comes up remains to be determined.

I will touch on the manias of foreign lending that occurred in 1808-10, 1823-25, 1856-61, 1885-90, 1910-13, and 1924-28 that were each followed by "revulsion"; along with the recycling of indemnity or reparation payments in 1819, 1871, and 1924, following the Napoleonic War, the Franco-Prussian War, and World War I, respectively. The boom lending of the first six periods was designed to increase productivity and hence should have carried its own mechanism for repayment; whereas reparation recycling comes much closer to consumption lending, which could be repaid only by reducing real income to achieve transfer.

These are, of course, ideal types, and the boom lending often had a number of similarities to consumption lending. The distinction is needed, however, to separate the type of long-term borrowing for productive uses which surged before the Yom Kippur War of November 1973, from the type of borrowing by many developing countries after that date, necessitated by the higher price of oil. At the same time, a considerable amount of the post-1973 borrowing was on behalf of nations belonging to OPEC, which were spending their increased revenue faster than it was being received. This OPEC borrowing, notably by Iran but also by Algeria, Libya, Nigeria, and Indonesia, strongly resembled the boom borrowing of the nineteenth century.

BOOM LOANS

Spurts of foreign lending can be found throughout the last 170 years. They were generally set off by some "displacement," to use the expression of Hyman Minsky, that is, an event or incident, a parametric shift or exogenous shock that draws attention to a new opportunity for profit. In 1808 the displacement was the Wellington campaign in the Iberian peninsula that caused the Portuguese royal family to leave for Brazil and led British merchants to send to Brazil in a few weeks as many goods as they had sent in the previous 20 years. In 1824-25, the boom in South American bonds followed the newly won independence from Spain to the Latin American colonies and the success of the Baring loan to finance the French indemnity payment to Britain. A boom in Turkey and Egypt in the 1860s followed the Crimean War and the European "cotton famine" of the American Civil War. A boom in Argentine securities after 1885 followed the government's reclamation of large tracts of rich land from the Indians in the south of that country and the offering of the land by the government for private sale on liberal terms. The peak of lending to Latin America occurred in 1911-13, from Britain, France, and Germany. Whether this would have led to a boom and bust cannot be known, as profits made by Latin American countries during World War I allowed all of the investment to be serviced and much of it to be paid off. In the 1920s the new lender, the New York market, was stimulated by the success of the Dawes loan, 11 times oversubscribed in 1924.

Following displacement, which provides a shift in horizon and draws attention to new or previously unnoticed opportunity, comes a wave of euphoria, as Minsky puts it, a rush to get in on the ground floor, sometimes a shift from investing for production to investing for capital gains. Often a group of insiders will buy in and later sell out to the outsiders when the boom has gone too far. In the imprecise but graphic words of Adam Smith, there is "overtrading," followed in many cases by "revulsion" and "discredit."

In the euphoric stage, promoters are to blame as much as the wildly optimistic and often profligate borrowers. Profits from good loans reaped by solid firms attract a marginal group that has to take risks to gain entry. In 1888 the Argentine government, according to W. Jett Lauck, was besieged by European promoters with proposals for railroads, docks, waterways, municipal improvements, and every description of public enterprise. In a speech in 1927, Thomas Lamont talked of hoards of American bankers and firms competing on an almost violent scale for the purpose of obtaining loans in various markets. At one time in Colombia in the 1920s there were 29 representatives of American houses using high-pressure methods on borrowers. In a chapter entitled "Klondike on the Nile," David S. Landes states that the real stake in Egyptian finance in the 1860s "lay in contracts and concessions for the construction of public works, the creation of public services, the exploitation of mineral resources, some legitimate . . . some frauds." The situation was analogous to the run during the last few years to the OPEC countries like Iran and Saudi Arabia, which became jammed with representatives of American, European, and Japanese businessmen and financiers.

Pitfalls of Boom Loans

While boom loans for projects were ostensibly for productive purposes that would provide the increased output with which to pay debt service (assuming the output was not diverted to consumption or to further investment), the higher the commissions, the lower the initial price, the more funds paid directly to foreign contractors who charged exorbitant prices, and the like, the more they resembled consumption loans. Some, in fact, were consumption loans to finance the deficits of governments or of the houses of monarchs. In 1868, for example, the viceroy of Egypt obtained £7 million in contracting for a debt of £12 million. The promoters turned a profit of £1.7 million. Yet, even the £7 million had no chance of being used productively by the viceroy, who loved yachts and palaces, since it was used to refund floating debt. The bankruptcy of the Egyptian government in 1876 and the consequent repudiation of foreign obligations were inevitable under these circumstances. Similarly, Max Winkler says, between 1859 and 1875, the Ottoman Empire borrowed abroad about $1 billion, of which only half was obtained in cash and only one-fifth of that used productively. Budgetary deficits continued through the boom generated by the Franco-Prussian indemnity to 1874, and bankruptcy ensured in the following depression in 1876.

Defaults of Boom Loans

Booms in foreign bond issues occur during periods of boom in business, and they come to a halt when business slacks off. An attempt may be made to sustain debt service for a time, and to complete construction projects underway, by shifting to short-term borrowing, but it will be short-lived. The New York banking houses that went down in September 1873, notably Jay Cooke & Co., failed because the railroads they were supporting with short-term loans were ultimately unable to pay service on any debt, long- or short-term. In June 1928, when the rise in interest rates made it impossible to sell foreign bonds, short-term lending continued for a brief period to the developing countries of Latin America, and for somewhat longer to Germany, which was borrowing for public works and indirectly to pay reparations. The shift from long- to short-term borrowing, however, and the urgent necessity to fund at unfavorable rates a rapidly rising floating debt, are both signs of "financial distress," defined by Myron J. Gordon as a "nontrivial probability," arising from a fall in a corporation's earnings power, that "it will not be able to pay the interest and principal on its debt."

Boom loans are undertaken on the upswing, defaulted at the peak, and refunded in the next upswing, which may also lead to new borrowing. Winkler reports on the default record of Guatemala, with borrowing in 1825, default in 1828, settlement in 1856, a new small loan in 1863, this defaulted in 1864, new loans in 1869, all loans defaulted in 1876, settlement in 1884, new loans in 1888, defaulted in 1894, new arrangement in 1895, that not carried out, new agreement in 1901-02, new agreement in 1903, new agreement in 1904, new loan in 1908, agreement of 1895 resumed in 1912, railway loan in 1924, new loans in 1927 and 1928, defaulted in 1931. He insists that the pattern represents the rule rather than the exception.

In short, productive loans in the developing countries are not very productive and do not stay long out of default, for several reasons: the lending occurs in bursts, often called "manias," which are precipitated, if not caused, by some shock to the system (the displacement), whipped up by euphoric excitement, overdone, with the borrower typically getting less than it is committed for and being forced to suspend debt service in the next recession.

This scenario was only partially true, however, of the really developing countries of the nineteenth century: the United States, Canada, Australia, South Africa, and New Zealand. It occurred in the Southern U.S. states which defaulted after borrowing in the Civil War. U.S. railroads also were overbuilt in booms, and went into receivership in recession, more or less regularly. British investment in land speculation in the United States in the 1830s, as well as in Argentina in the 1880s, was largely dissipated in consumption. But the United States and the Dominions were really, and not merely euphemistically, "developing"; they were competent in transforming resources from the domestic to the foreign-trade sector (for exports and to compete with imports). In Latin America, the Middle East, and czarist Russia, cyclical borrowing was followed by cyclical default, partly because of the awkward terms under which the hapless debtors borrowed—particularly the Ottoman Empire and Egypt—but primarily because development never got thoroughly underway.

CONSUMPTION LOANS

Borrowing for consumption is normally a legitimate exercise for those with assets—the rich—or those whose earning power is assuredly rising. For the poor with uncertain prospects it has the disadvantage of providing no increase in output from which debt service can be undertaken, and the borrower's poverty provides little cushion from which the debt service can be squeezed. The most miserable debtor is the Indian peasant who in famine must borrow in order to eat, and then must borrow further in normal times in order to pay interest on his debt. He has no prospect of escaping the burden of continuously rising debt.

Reparations are like consumption loans and can be paid internationally only if there is a cushion for compressing the standard of living, and the country owing the reparations takes steps—either voluntarily or under threat of force—to achieve that compression. It is also possible to gain time in effecting payment by recycling, that is, by borrowing money to make the payments and then later paying off that debt.

There is an interesting contrast between France's reparations payment in 1871 and Germany's failure to pay the reparations due under the Versailles treaty following World War I. The French were eager to get German troops out of France following the Franco-Prussian War. They wished to discharge their international obligation, and to turn to other concerns like colonization in North Africa. After an initial payment in specie of about 10 percent, they recycled the debt by borrowing at home, welcoming foreign subscriptions, and encouraging subscribers to sell foreign assets. In effect, France transferred to Germany 500 million francs in gold plus 4.5 million francs in France's foreign assets. The subsequent reconstitution of these investments by French investors was the real transfer of currently produced goods and services.

Germany, on the other hand, had little will to work to pay its reparations. Keynes's polemic, *The Economic Consequences of the Peace*, helped to convince the Germans that they had been cruelly treated. In the earliest stages, payments were made with funds which flowed in from abroad to take advantage of the depreciation of the mark, so long as the world had inelastic expectations and believed that the mark would return to par. (A recent paper by Carl-Ludwig Holtfrerich makes the point that Germany got more help from abroad through these private charitable and speculative inflows in 1919–23 than West Germany received under the Marshall Plan after World War II.)

Recycling worked effectively to stretch out reparations in 1819 and in 1871. In 1924 and 1930, with the Dawes and Young loans, it merely transferred the losses on ultimate default from reparation recipients to buyers of German bonds.

Recycling also can occur through selling outstanding assets in a third market, or by not renewing foreign bonds as they mature and requiring the debtor to refund them in a third market. The outstanding episodes of these forms of recycling relate to Germany in the 1880s. A domestic boom, and concern about the value of Argentine bonds, led German investors to dump their holdings in the British market, damaging it and contributing to the ultimate failure of Baring Brothers which had underwritten issues it was unable to market. The initiative for recycling may also come partly from the debtor. During this same period, Germany turned away from Russian bonds and, as issues matured in Germany, refunded them in the French market, leaving that country stuck when default came in 1917.

A similar shifting of the lending burden occurred early in the borrowing caused by the OPEC price hike. U.S. banks in the Eurodollar market stopped lending to Italy, which then requested a $5 billion loan without collateral from the European Economic Community, but had to be satisfied with a $2 billion loan from Germany with gold collateral. On the whole, however, once Saudi Arabia and Kuwait had recycled to the Eurocurrency market the loans needed to continue oil consumption, there was little prospect that much of the debt could be recycled further along.

It is a well-known Latin American complaint that the developed countries take more money out of the area than they put in, meaning that new loans and investments typically amount to less than interest and dividends, remitted depreciation, depletion, and amortization on old investment. The complaint is justified as far as depreciation, depletion, and amortization are concerned. If these exceed new loans, gross capital is flowing from, rather than to, Latin America. Comparing interest and dividends with new loans, net of depreciation and amortization, however, is typically fallacious. Interest and dividends on old investments should be paid by the productivity of those investments. To think otherwise is akin to saying that a man with ten shares of General Motors stock has some moral obligation to invest his dividends each year in General Motors (perhaps on the automatic dividend reinvestment plan). On this reasoning, any investment, once made, must continue to eternity and can never yield income to be spent.

The complaint could, however, be justified in the case of consumption loans where there is no productivity from which interest and dividends can be earned and income is so low that consumption and investment cannot be compressed to yield a margin for debt service. Loans for productive purposes that are dissipated in commissions and supplier profits, and which yield only a small fraction of their value in producing assets, are like consumption loans for the purpose of this comparison. In these cases, interest must be added to principal each year in new loans, quite apart from still further loans to cover the next year's consumption; and the lending countries should put more in new loans each year than they take out in interest, dividends, and capital allowances.

DEFAULT

From the history of the 30 years since World War II, the impression can readily be gained that default on international obligations is rare. The Paris Club meets only occasionally to deal with a case and is successful in rescheduling payments to avoid the impression, but not the reality, of substantial default. Ghana, following the reckless spending of Nkrumah, or Indonesia, after Sukarno, submitted to the treatment and started off again. But such cases are few. Economists resort to fairly sophisticated statistical methods like discriminate analysis to determine under what circumstances of debt-service ratios, accumulated indebtedness, rate of increase of income, and the like the limited cases of default have occurred.

The historical record of the 100-plus years from the Napoleonic period to World War II, however, suggests that default was much more frequent. It was on the basis of that record that Leon Frazer of the First National Bank of New York and one-time president of the Bank for International Settlements said it was better to have loaned and lost than never to have loaned at all. Historically, euphoria and reckless lending, with great waste of resources, almost inevitably led to default. Only in the case of the United States and the British Dominions, despite substantial waste, were productive investments undertaken that led to substantial economic growth.

In the present circumstances, apart from the OPEC countries, there has been little euphoria in foreign lending. European lending to Eastern Europe and the Soviet Union, in typical disregard of the Berne convention designed to moderate it, constitutes another exception and so, to a limited extent, does the flurry in the period of cheap money from the end of 1971 to November 1973. The problem of developing-country debt today is rather that the loans to developing countries, and even those to Britain, France, and Italy since 1973, have been used to finance consumption, and that the recycling which has postponed default cannot be continued indefinitely.

Whether consumption will be reduced enough to free up domestic resources (to reduce imports and expand exports) and so effectively transfer interest and ultimately reduce principal is largely a political question, just as it was with German reparations after World War I. The fiscal policy required to produce the budgetary surplus, and the monetary policy needed to assist fiscal policy in converting a budget surplus into a current-account surplus in the balance of payments, will reduce the consumption or investment of particular groups. If all affected groups resist such reduction, interest on consumption loans cannot be raised at home to be transferred abroad. The game can be sustained without growth only by adding the interest to the principal each year.

I am not sanguine about the developing countries' current prospects for depressing consumption and investment adequately to raise, out of current levels of income, the wherewithal to pay debt service on their accumulated debt. The problem has been exacerbated by the fact that the oil-price hike, which gave rise to consumption loans, also touched off a world recession. Maintaining debt service during world depression is generally impossible. Where countries have made serious efforts to do so—in Germany until the standstill agreement of July 1931 and in the Soviet Union with its relatively small debts through the 1930s—the results have been thoroughly unsatisfactory: the rise of totalitarianism out of mass unemployment on the one hand, and mass starvation through diversion of grain from cities to exports on the other.

The debt service on the euphoric lending to the OPEC countries can probably readily be handled, but the Iranian experience has already demonstrated the necessity for some sobering-up in this arena. The requisite for avoidance of defaults by other developing countries, which would have repercussions on the world financial mechanism, is a resumption of the world economic recovery which began at the end of 1975 and suffered a pause in the second portion of 1976. A rising tide floats, if not all boats, at least those that are not riddled with holes.

THE LENDER OF LAST RESORT

When default does occur, the historical record demonstrates the value of a lender of last resort, both nationally and internationally. Yet the role is an ambiguous one at best. If a lender of last resort is known to exist, it relaxes discipline and incentive in the system. In other words, if you know that somebody is going to come to the rescue, then there is no need for you to go to all the trouble to be prudent. And if there is no lender of last resort in the final analysis, then deflation rolls through the system. The depression in 1929 was so long, so wide, and so deep because there was no lender of last resort in the system at that time.

For a central bank to come forward too early is to encourage undisciplined lending, and to wait too long is to induce spreading collapse. The domino metaphor may or may not be applicable to small country wars; it applies well to spreading bankruptcy and default. This is a lesson learned by the Bank of England at the national level in the eighteenth century, according to T. S. Ashton, and at the international level in the twentieth century. On occasion, as in 1839 and 1890, the Bank of England sought help from the Bank of France, the Hamburg Bank, and the Russian government, and once the Bank of France assisted Britain by providing specie, whether or not it was asked for.

Today, after the Herstatt and Franklin affairs, it seems evident that central banks constitute the lenders of last resort for domestic institutions, to prevent repercussions of domestic failure and disruption from spreading abroad, as the world so patently failed to do in 1929 and especially 1931.

Former Chairman Arthur F. Burns of the Board of Governors of the Federal Reserve System and Congressman Henry S. Reuss of the Joint Economic Committee of the U.S. Congress have insisted publicly that the United States is not the lender of last resort on an international basis, and that the role should be borne by the International Monetary Fund (IMF). I see dangers in this viewpoint. The IMF cannot act rapidly, as its directors must seek instructions. In crises, the Bank for International Settlements, usually at the initiative of the United States, has been able to act immediately and the IMF, as a rule, has followed along and consolidated whatever help did not unwind itself after the crisis.

It would be intolerable if a crisis were to break out and require international rather than domestic action by a lender of last resort to stand, as in May, June, and July 1931, and debate what sort of action should be taken and by whom. Academics and journalists on the outside need not be privy to contingency plans, yet I would like to think that there is some contingency plan which is not being revealed. Crises present themselves in new guises each time, so that greatly detailed planning with differing scenarios is not likely to be useful.

I find myself in sympathy in this matter with a view expressed by Sir Robert Peel when the Bank Act of 1844 was being debated in the House of Commons and the question was raised about whether advance provision should be made for contingencies. Sir Robert's opinion was thus expressed: "If it be necessary to assume a grave responsibility, I dare say men will be found willing to assume such a responsibility." Sir Robert's dictum proved correct for Britain in the nineteenth century. Let us hope that it applies to the United States and to the world in the last quarter of the twentieth century.

2

HOW MUCH PRIVATE BANK
LENDING IS ENOUGH?
Henry C. Wallich

Under the narrow umbrella of the title of this chapter, I hope to consider three topics:

1. Some general observations about the OPEC surplus and the difficulties associated with any bank lending to developing countries.
2. Country risk analysis as a guide to lending policy.
3. Some bank regulatory innovations.

My principal conclusions will be:

Some slowing of the rate of total borrowing of some countries should occur, as well as an increase in the relative share of official lending in total international financing, but the main burden of financing must continue to be carried by private institutions and markets.

The banks are very active in improving their techniques of country analysis. Further progress needs to be made, nevertheless, especially toward coordination of procedures and definitions. More information also will have to be obtained on borrowing countries' economies and finances, through the cooperation of these countries themselves, and official financial institutions.

The regulatory authorities will have to develop techniques that will allow bank examiners to comment on risks taken in foreign lending without doing irreparable damage to the credit standing of particular countries.

THE OPEC SURPLUS AND LENDING TO DEVELOPING COUNTRIES

To avoid the gloom often associated with the presentation of large numbers, I would like to begin with a positive point. The OPEC surplus, despite all the trouble it is giving us, nevertheless has the potential for increased investment and growth if it is channeled properly. By taxing the world without consuming (or investing at home) the full revenue, OPEC is putting investable resources at the disposal of the rest of the world. So far the reduction in purchasing power brought about by the tax has caused mainly unemployment. But the potentially positive effect, of perhaps $45 billion in 1977, should not be altogether ignored.

The way to take advantage of this opportunity is not by general economic stimulation, which would be inflationary, but through selective tax measures designed to favor the channeling of available savings into investment. In the longer term, I believe, the demand for investable funds will be strong in any event.

Second, a word of moderate encouragement concerning the position of the non-oil-producing developing countries: Contrary to a widespread belief, it does not appear that the entire massive OPEC-induced deficit has been shifted to these countries. When allowance is made for changes in export and import prices, the deficits of the non-oil-producing developing countries today are about what a projection of their trends during 1965-72 would indicate. Their debt-service ratios, over the last few years, have not significantly deteriorated in the aggregate. Of course, this does not apply to every country, nor does it offer a basis for complacency with respect to the future evolution of debt-service burdens as grace periods end and, possibly, the LIBOR (London InterBank Offering Rate), upon which syndicated bank loan rates are based, rises. In any case, it must be borne in mind that developing countries are structural capital importers whose total debt is almost certain to rise over time, even though individual obligations are serviced punctually.

Third, the OPEC nations, broadly speaking, have replaced the major industrial countries as the principal suppliers of international capital. Where previously the industrial countries functioned as net lenders (and grantors), their surplus going to the developing countries, today their role has shifted. Financial institutions in the industrial countries currently are intermediating between OPEC nations in surplus and developing countries in deficit.

Fouth, the smaller industrial countries, and a number of other developed countries, have experienced deficits that would not have been predicted from their earlier behavior or their structural characteristics. It may well be that the main problems of financing in the future will have to be confronted by some of the countries in this group.

Fifth, the relative inadequacy of balance-of-payments adjustment so far is reflected in the fact that the effective real exchange rates, in many countries that have floating rates, have not changed significantly. Effective nominal rates have changed, more or less in line with differential rates of national inflations. But international competitiveness among major countries has not changed a great deal, since nominal exchange-rate movements mainly reflect changes in purchasing power parity.

Today it has become fashionable to talk of the OPEC-induced deficits as a burden in a twofold sense. One sense relates to the burden of the real resources transfer required to eliminate a deficit. The higher-priced oil has to be paid for by an increase in exports or by a cut in imports, which means diminished availability of goods at home. The other sense relates to the burden of financing the deficits, to the extent that they are not eliminated by the first route. In other words, we are talking about the burdens of not financing the deficits and of financing them. In this vale of tears, everything seems to be a burden. But we should not overlook the fact that to the extent a country shoulders one burden it reduces the other.

Today, concern is primarily focused upon the burden of financing. Thinking runs along the line of allocating current account deficits, with the intention of making the debt burden more readily bearable. This makes good financial sense. But we must nevertheless remember that there is another side to the matter. The "minimum financial burden" criterion requires that the strongest and richest countries reduce their surpluses or go into large deficits. This is not what economists had in mind when they developed the proposition that capital should flow to the areas where its marginal product is highest. Structurally, the strongest and richest countries should expect to be capital exporters. Instead, the requirements of financial balance may cause the United States to become a capital importer.

Under these conditions the issue of greater safety for financing and more efficient allocation of capital becomes a trade-off. The decision must be a political one. To the extent that the nations of the world prefer a more efficient allocation of capital, the ensuing higher risks will have to be borne predominately by official lenders. The banks, when they lend to finance capital movements, must lean toward safety. And the greater the share of the overall financing job assigned to them, the more the financing will have to go toward the stronger and safer countries.

In this context, there is no good answer to the question, "How much bank lending is enough," any more than to the question of whether enough is too much, or whether perhaps, as Mark Twain said about whiskey, too much is barely enough. It all depends on to whom, and in what form, the lending goes. Banks are very much aware of these problems and most have integrated country risk analysis into their international lending decisions. I would, therefore, like to say a few words about the subject of country risk.

COUNTRY RISK ANALYSIS AS A GUIDE TO LENDING POLICY

The analysis of country risk involves two major topics: the definition and measurement of exposure, and the examination and assessment of the risk factors presented by particular countries.

With respect to the former, the Federal Reserve System has been engaged in an informal and preliminary survey of bank practices and capabilities. This survey, which has been conducted in a structured interview form, has produced some interesting results. On the whole, the banks are doing an effective job of monitoring and analyzing their foreign-country exposure. There are, however, a significant number of differences in the treatment of particular forms of exposure. One of the most significant differences in country risk measurement involves the allocation of interbank placements, which can be considered as exposure associated with either the country of the banking office in which the deposit is placed, because activities in that country might affect repayment; or the country of the head office of the banking office accepting the deposit, because the depositing bank is looking to the parent institution as the ultimate source of repayment.

Another difference arises in allocating exposure on shipping loans, where the owner may not be a citizen of the same country in which the ship is registered. To make things more complicated, the loan may be secured by a charter to a company which holds its assets in a third country, or perhaps multinationally. A further difference concerns the treatment of intrabank transactions and whether these transactions, which are netted out in preparing consolidated balance sheets for a bank, affect foreign exposure. When intrabank transactions are included in country exposure measures, the total foreign exposure of the bank may well exceed its total foreign portfolio. Still another difference involves the treatment of local loans. Is country risk exposure affected when a bank's foreign branch funds its local country loans through local deposits?

In addition to these questions, many of which perhaps ought to be resolved by allocating the risk to all countries whose policies might affect the exposure, consideration needs to be given to differences in the degree of exposure resulting from different forms of commitment. Bank placements do not involve the same degree of risk as medium-term loans. Short-term export credits are more self-liquidating, in foreign-exchange terms, than short-term import credits. Medium-term loans to, or guaranteed by, an official agency of the borrower country may be safer than those to private parties.

More important than these issues pertaining to the treatment of risk within the bank's decision framework is the analysis of the economic, financial, and political situation of the individual debtor country. Practitioners of this activity are the first to point out that anlaysis of country risk is not a science. I hesitate to call it an art; perhaps it may be dignified with the term "craft."

A number of familiar ratios and relationships exist which throw light on the ability of a country to service, or allow its residents to service, foreign indebtedness. The ability to service foreign debt is positively related to the level of exports and, not quite so closely, to gross national product (GNP). In the very short run, it is directly related to the level of reserves and to available credit facilities. It is positively related also to the "compressibility" of imports, which, in turn, tends to be a function of per capita GNP and of the composition of imports.

But these are very partial relationships. In some of them the variables are not even accurately defined. Far more subtle and detailed relationships and data can and need to be brought to bear on the problem. Even then, different views may be supported by the same basic facts.

Finally, the behavior of debtor countries cannot be expected to be altogether independent of one another. If one country were to suspend service on its debts, others might follow. The reaction of lenders to the first default might be to deprive other borrowers of credit. The onus of default also might appear less great to the second than to the first. The very limited cases of rescheduling since 1970 however, produce such a domino effect.

REGULATORY AND SUPERVISORY ACTION

Three important areas invite the attention of bank regulators when they focus upon international bank lending: the need for adequate information, IMF policy with respect to conditionality, and the proper role of country risk analysis in bank supervision and examination. With respect to information, very considerable efforts are being made by banks today to keep themselves fully informed of all developments affecting the countries to or in which they lend. This, at any rate, appears to be the present case of the lead banks in syndicated loans. Banks that participate in loans without ever taking the lead are sometimes less active in seeking information. Nevertheless, "investigate before you invest" applies to syndicate participation just as much as to stock-exchange investments, although the costs of acquiring that information may be high for banks planning limited participation in a credit. Each bank must consider every loan in relation to its own special circumstances. What is good for a leading money-market bank, which is interested in developing collateral or possibly in getting approval to open a branch, is not necessarily good for a medium-sized regional bank which has limited contact with the borrower.

Better information can be provided if commercial banks are able to draw on data supplied by borrowing countries to international institutions such as the International Monetary Fund (IMF), the Bank for International Settlements (BIS), and the World Bank. Questions of confidentiality may impose limits on what these institutions can communicate to private parties. Nevertheless, through the intervention of central banks, and perhaps best through the authorization of the country in question, part of this difficulty can be bridged.

But the confidential character of some of the available information is not really the essence of the matter. More fundamental is the fact that information that ought to be readily available simply does not exist either at the public or confidential level for the simple reason that it has not been collected. Data on total indebtedness, including private debt, the maturity profile of this total indebtedness, and the interest burden thereon, often are simply unknown. Countries that maintain exchange controls certainly ought to be able to collect this type of information. Countries without controls could make a greater effort to approximate such data by statistical rather than regulatory methods. In short, the fundamental point often is not the inaccessibility of banks to data that are known to official agencies, but that the data are simply unknown to anybody.

I now turn to the IMF's conditionality. By this I mean the IMF's practice of conditioning access to some of its credit to the establishment by the borrowing country of certain economic and financial policies. It has been argued that the IMF should play a greater role in private bank lending, through the negotiation of standby loan aggreements, followed perhaps by cofinancing with commercial banks. I believe that this is a promising approach. At the same time, we should recognize that commercial banks can establish some kind of conditionality even without the help of the IMF. Where a country has continuing relationships with major banks or expects to come to the market with some frequency, the banks' counsel on domestic policies will have an influence, without implying any lack of respect for the country's sovereignty. By paying out a loan in installments, contingent on performance reviews, private banks can influence a country's willingness to follow agreed policies, even in the absence of a binding contract. On the other hand, the IMF's power to influence a country's policies through the conditionality of its lending is not unlimited. National governments face domestic political realities that they cannot, in an effort to conciliate the IMF, ignore without danger to social and political stability.

What matters is that commercial banks and international institutions act in coordination with each other. The borrowing country should not be able to look to the banks as a means of circumventing the conditionality that the IMF has attempted to establish. The banks, on the other hand, should not look to the IMF as a bail-out from injudicious loans.

At the level of bank supervision, I would like to stress the great importance of maintaining bank soundness and safety without injuring the credit of debtor countries. Classification of bank loans that the examiner wishes to criticize as "substandard," "doubtful," "loss," and "special mention," is a useful supervisory practice at home. We are all aware of the problems that use of the same technique internationally may produce. The impression that occasionally has arisen abroad, that examiners have classified entire countries, instead of particular loans to borrowers located in those countries, can have unfortunate consequences.

Consideration might be given to an alternative approach that would focus the bank examination of foreign loans on the degree of concentration of such loans in particular countries. Criticism of concentration in an industry or area is a normal feature of bank examination, due attention being given of course to the nature of each bank's market area. If such a procedure were to be applied to foreign lending, no country would be altogether deprived of access to bank credit, and individually sound loans would still be made available. Under such an approach, no country would be classified as a strong or weak credit risk, although there could be distinctions between stronger and weaker credit risks within countries. Concentration also might be defined, as it is domestically, with respect to the share of a bank's capital exposed to a particular country risk.

This procedure would give the examining authorities a means of coming to grips with weak foreign risks and excessive bank exposure without damaging the credit standing of an individual country or depriving a country of bank credit altogether. It should be noted, in this context, that a bank's awareness that a particular loan will be "classified" by an examiner does not legally prevent the bank from making that loan. If the bank has reason to believe that the loan is appropriate, it may decide to make it even though its examination report will be adversely affected.

In conclusion, I would like to stress that, with respect to foreign lending, the role of the bank supervisory authorities today is a delicate one. There is need for increased caution and restraint. There is need also for continued bank lending to countries where risk is acceptable. Bank supervisors must seek to control excessive exposure without damaging the international flow of capital. Excessive restrictions, by possibly impeding necessary roll-overs as well as desirable new capital inflows, would be counterproductive and could possibly provoke the defaults that bank supervision seeks to guard against. It might also discourage banks only marginally involved in foreign lending from continuing that activity, thereby placing an additional burden on large banks and increasing their concentration in foreign lending. Success in walking the fine line between too much and too little caution will be essential not only to the safety of the U.S. banking system but also to the prosperity of the United States and of the entire world.

EMERGING ROLE
OF PRIVATE BANKS
Irving S. Friedman

I would like to highlight certain points that are made in greater detail elsewhere in the proceedings. I will not particularly argue them, but I believe they are worth reviewing and discussing.

ROLE OF PRIVATE BANKS

One point is the conclusion that private banks will continue to be an important source of financing for many developing countries. What we have seen is not a temporary phenomenon. The private banks are now an important or major source of financing only for a minority of the developing countries, but the number of developing countries that will be borrowing from the private banks will grow steadily.

There will be important shifts, however, in the relative importance of these countries in the total portfolio of the private banks. The banks should be constrained in lending to some countries by their already substantial exposure. (Henry Wallich in his contribution makes a very important point and very interesting suggestion in this regard, which could be a guiding point for the regulatory authorities.) The point is that the banks should be constrained by the so-called actuarial principle, which is simply not having too many eggs in one basket.

Second, the reasons that private banks will continue to be an important source of financing can be found both on the demand side—from the borrowers, that is, the developing countries—and on the supply side—in the ability of private banks to respond in adequate amounts and on acceptable financial terms, combined with the continued inadequacies of official sources of external financing for the developing countries.

The discussion of this subject is sometimes confused by the failure to recognize that the response of the banks is the response to a demand. Bankers do not make loans to countries, or to entities within countries, that do not ask them for a loan. The fact is that someone comes to a bank and asks for a loan. Then the banker judges whether to do it. Banks compete for attractive loans, but the borrower is essentially the genesis of the loan.

Third, the reasons for borrowing from the private banks are not to be found in the easier conditions than the IMF, nor are they to be found in the existence of the OPEC surpluses. Here I would like to emphasize that some of these points are fairly controversial, with considerable differences in points of view.

The main point, however, is that the developing countries do not borrow from the private banks to delay the adjustment process they would otherwise undertake. I will come back to this in the discussion of lending standards.

One of the most confusing ideas we have had to contend with in this field is the linkage of the OPEC surpluses with the financing of the deficits of developing countries. This is very tempting because of its simplicity and its elegance. I am not talking about what causes the developing countries to have a deficit but, rather, the mechanism of financing their deficits which is now seen as a linkage, and to which we now have applied the term "recycling."

This view is expressed by many analysts. The essential idea is that, together with the acceptance of deposits from OPEC surplus countries, what we are seeing is the on-lending of these surpluses to developing countries. Expanding on this, I may draw a very crude analogy to purchases of U.S. government bonds by the OPEC countries. I do not hear the U.S. Treasury saying to deficit countries when a certain country or group of countries has purchased a certain amount of bonds, "Please let us give you loans." That is not too crude an analogy of what actually is said to happen in the world's private banking system. What the banks have are deposits of which only a small part represents oil surpluses. On the other hand, the banks have lending opportunities in developing countries which, among other things, are caused by the high price of oil. Then we have the question of how they are financed. They are not financed by the oil surplus deposits. They are financed by the credit-extending capacity of the banks, which greatly exceeds oil deposits.

LENDING STANDARDS

Another point I heard is that one of the reasons we have seen an expansion of private lending is a lowering of private bank lending standards. This is frequently attributed to the slack demand for bank credit in the United States, matched by a similar slack demand in other Western countries. Usually, however, the emphasis is appropriately placed on the United States, because the United States is by far the largest single source of private bank lending. It is sometimes said that the private banks are "reaching" for loans. This is a concept which is often found, even in periodicals which are considered friendly to the private banks. I do not think it is right.

Let me make a few points that are on the other side and that are equally in dispute. It is obvious to me, from the perspective of long experience in the IMF and the World Bank, that private banks must have more cautious, broader, and more stringent lending criteria than either the IMF or the World Bank. If one thinks for a moment about the private character of these banks, it is easy to deduce why it is that a private bank is essentially a very cautious lender. This is true whether you think in terms of shareholders, of banks' liabilities to their depositors, or whether you think of their other liabilities or their outstanding indebtedness.

A private bank has to be a more cautious lender than any international institution whose aims and objectives are not those of a private institution. The objectives of the international institution may include the defense of the international monetary system. Its objectives may be to help a member country to maintain certain levels of employment, to bring down certain rates of inflation, or to achieve other domestic economic goals that are considered desirable. Its objectives may also include certain kinds of balance-of-payments targets like removal of restrictions or multiple currency practices. These objectives are not those of a commercial bank. Therefore, the criteria for lending by these institutions inevitably reflect the purposes for which they are established—and also reflect the source of their funding. The fact is that their funding is either directly from governments, as in the case of the IMF, or indirectly from governments and from private investors, as in the case of the World Bank. Risk of repayment is secondary to their primary purposes. The advice given, or even conditions imposed, are not primarily designed to make repayment possible, though they may well help to do so.

I would maintain, therefore, with the experience that I have had, that private bank borrowing by the developing countries has frequently accelerated their need for adjustment. I could mention Zaire, Peru has been mentioned, and I can give you many examples of this during 1975 and 1976. If anything, the concern ought to be that the adjustment process, if it continues with an overdependence on the private banks, can become too severe and can become too quick. The private banks do not have a mandate to be anything except very cautious.

Think for a moment of what the world would look like without the IMF and the World Bank. If developing countries had only the private banks to turn to, the so-called adjustment process would have been much quicker, and much more disruptive.

Another point I would like to make, even more controversial from some points of view, is that monitoring by someone outside the country is a sign of weakness, whether done by the IMF or anyone else. The idea that monitoring strengthens a country is only logical if one is describing a country that is already perceived as weak. Now, if a country is already perceived as poorly managed, then there is no doubt that monitoring by the IMF is a plus, as the monitoring agent has a reputation for achieving better country management.

On the other hand, we should be very careful not to slip into a way of thinking in which the monitoring itself is perceived as giving strength. What gives the country strength is that the monitoring gives reason to believe that the government is going to change its economic policies. Therefore, what we are going to see is an improvement in the economic management of the country, as compared with the previous situation which was perceived as one of poor economic management. However, I maintain that, in the case of countries that are well managed, the concept of monitoring can be a very difficult concept. It can even be damaging to the country, as well as damaging to the functioning of the international monetary system.

RELATIONSHIPS WITH FUND AND BANK

I believe, and I would like to stress, that the IMF can judge the adequacy or appropriateness of fiscal, monetary, and foreign exchange-rate policies, as well as the adequacy or appropriateness of external payment restrictions and other balance-of-payments policies. If this is done technically and nonpolitically, which essentially is the way the IMF does it, it can make a very important contribution to the decision-making process of the private banks. However, if the IMF is to make the greatest contribution, it should coordinate its recommendations with the development institutions. We cannot have a judgment by the IMF only, unless the IMF redefines its area of concern; the IMF is too narrow from the point of view of a private bank. Coordinating with the World Bank may be the hardest thing in the world to do. On the other hand, if the two of them can get together, they would then, in my opinion, be better able to judge what is good management (my World Bank colleagues will understand when I say that the World Bank may include the Asian Development Bank, Inter-American Development Bank, and so on). What is regarded as good economic management must encompass the entire range of economic management in the country, rather than just taking out one part of it and labeling it "economic management."

The point of view of the private banks is that they must be kept up to date. It does not do one much good to know what was thought about a country six months ago. One has to know what one thinks about the subject *today*, because today is the day one is going to make a loan. Banking is a continuous process based on up-to-date information of the best available quality. The official institutions should try to think through how they might be more coordinated with the private banking sector. They could make an important contribution if they would do this.

There can be no ambiguity as to the availability of information and judgments on a current basis. If—and this has happened to me repeatedly—at the last minute you are told, "We are sorry but we have just decided we cannot give you certain information because the executive directors have not yet considered it,"

I thoroughly understand. The scope of the limitations, however, must be known in advance. If it is understood that certain information is not available, then it is not available. There should be no ambiguity as to what can be given, what cannot be given, and when the material which can be given can definitely be made available. In this regard, the same rule ought to apply to the World Bank, to the U.S. Commerce Department, and so forth.

PRIVATE BANK INFORMATION

The private banks have to go considerably beyond the World Bank and the IMF in analyzing country creditworthiness. I have a list of areas of private bank concern or knowledge about a country that one would not expect the IMF or the World Bank to know. One cannot expect an international organization to go into many aspects of the economy that directly impinge a foreign private bank operating abroad or directly impinge the customer base that a foreign private bank has within a country, any more than any private bank would investigate the details of a project as the World Bank does.

The private banks have no choice in today's world. They must know the countries into which they are lending extremely well, in depth, and on a continuing basis. The only way this choice can be avoided is by making one of these three prior decisions:

We will not lend into the country in any important amounts; therefore, we simply do not have to know the country well, because the total amount of lending into that country is not going to be significant from the point of view of our overall portfolio, our capital, or reserves.

We are going to rely on others; that is, we are only going to lend abroad when we are part of a syndication. We are going to be very careful in probing members of that syndication; we are going to make sure that the agent banks know the borrowing countries well and we are going to rely on their judgments.

We will rely on a correspondent bank relationship. We will, in effect, rely upon our correspondent banks for the judgments about countries, because that is one of the services we are going to give each other.

The international banking community has access to information in extraordinary depth and breadth. Their knowledge of countries is often much greater than that of any other institution. The problem which still has to be resolved is the extent to which the private banks can share their information with each other without raising problems of an antitrust nature with the regulatory authorities. Within the past two years, the private banks have done more and more talking to each other. Some private banks have been able to offset each other's weaknesses by sharing information. Some banks will be very strong in some countries, not so strong in others. Some banks will be very strong in terms of their knowledge about the multinationals and others will be strong in their knowledge about governments. Other banks will be strong on domestic corporations. There is a tremendous pool of knowledge that I see every day among the international banks.

In effect, what we are seeing is a mechanism being formed, within the legal constraints, which allows the private international banks to share their information with each other and with those that do not have their capabilities. I think that private international banks will continue to play a major role as lenders. Given this, I believe that the principal impact of the information sharing will be that banks will be able to assess countries more adequately. This will heighten the confidence in their ability to lend abroad prudently. They will accept the need for self-reliance in making judgments on countries. They will welcome information from whatever source is available. Borrowing countries will become increasingly familiar with the judgments and criteria of the lending institutions. As a consequence, the economic management of the developing countries is inevitably going to be influenced more and more by the criteria of private bank lending.

DEBT SITUATION OF THE DEVELOPING
COUNTRIES AND FUTURE PROSPECTS

4

THE DEVELOPING-COUNTRY
DEBT SITUATION

Anthony M. Solomon

I would like to offer a few comments on my own perceptions on the debt question. Basically, there are three main themes:

Debt problems are, of course, a manifestation of, and a part of, broader economic and financial problems. Undue concentration on debt per se does not provide the right perspective for the development of governmental policy to deal with fundamental problems that may ultimately boil over and become explicit as debt problems. It's simply a way of describing a troublesome payments deficit. A country's response to the deficit need not be to default or reschedule debt. It can reduce its deficit in other ways: through curbing domestic demand, depreciation of the exchange rate, or trade restrictions.

The debt problem and its underlying causes are not exclusively, or even mainly, a developing-country problem. Again, the focus is, in a sense, misleading. It tends to produce proposals or demands on the part of developing countries for action that not only will not address fundamental causes of problems, but also will ignore some countries that face the most difficult debt problems. The North/South framework is simply not the right framework.

Although I do not pretend to know or even be aware of all the data now collected and disseminated, my impression is that there are great gaps in the information available to private lenders and to governments on borrowers' debt positions, financial situations, and economic policies. It seems clear and inevitable that this situation is going to have to improve, and that improvement is in the interest of lenders and borrowers—or at least prudent borrowers—alike.

ACCUMULATION OF DEBT

Accumulation of debt is, of course, a product of other factors, other problems; nevertheless, the scale of debt accumulation has grown vastly since the

1973-74 oil price increases, and this has attracted a great deal of attention and concern. But there are a number of points to be made here. Even though the financing and debt numbers have grown enormously in the past few years, they are not grossly off-scale. A very partial look—concentrated on the developing countries, in part, because the World Bank has made major debt-collection efforts here and the data are better than for the more advanced countries—indicates: projected developing-country deficits for 1977 are about the same as the average for 1972, when adjusted for inflation and real growth; debt-service ratios actually declined between 1971 and 1975, although there was a slight increase in 1976. Because we don't have a good maturity profile, we don't know exactly what this may imply for the future, but it takes some of the bite out of the alarm that might be caused by the massive absolute figures.

Morgan Guaranty, in December 1976, attempted to normalize current account deficits to take account of growth in the world economy and inflation. Results showed that the developing-country deficits in 1976-77 were close to historic norms, while the industrialized country deficits were quite large relative to norm. This indicates that the industrialized countries have undertaken more of the burden.

Debt is going to have to continue to accumulate in absolute terms at a fairly rapid pace. And, as we all know, the OPEC surplus, notwithstanding President Carter's energy proposals, is not going to disappear overnight. We expect an aggregate OPEC surplus on the order of $45 billion again in 1978. Although we hope for moderation in future years, there is no radical change in sight on the horizon.

Nor are imbalances within country groups going to disappear. Some of the OECD* countries are running current account surpluses. Some of the OPEC countries are running current account deficits. Aggregating the deficits of all countries we expect to be in deficit—admittedly on fairly static assumptions—we see total potential net financing needs on the order of $67 billion in 1977.

The money exists to finance these international imbalances. If it did not, the imbalances could not realistically be projected. The oil exporters do not bury their money in the sand any more eagerly than U.S. exporters do. If it is not spent, it is lent or invested.

Thus the real question is whether countries that need financing will be in a position to attract it. This is a very narrow question in the sense that it demands very specific assessments of, and answers about, individual countries, not generalizations about groups of countries. It is also very broad, in that, if the answer is no, then we face drastic changes in the international economic system. In the individual country's case, the question is whether the country's policies engender confidence that debt will be repaid. And the question of policy, not the level of debt per se, is the question I feel we have to focus on.

---

*Organization for Economic Cooperation and Development.

FOCUS ON DEVELOPING COUNTRIES

I don't want to spend too much time on my second main point: whether the focus on developing countries is right in considering debt; most of my views on this are already evident from my earlier comments. But it is worth saying that of all the financing problems I can now anticipate, relatively few are in the developing countries, and in absolute financial terms those few developing-country problems are not massive and should be manageable with the right policies on the part of the countries concerned. Developing-country reserves rose by $10 billion in 1976. This points to creditworthiness, and to a possible decline in borrowing in 1977, since borrowing financed reserve increases in 1976.

Unfortunately, as I said earlier, the framework we have allowed ourselves to get into has cast the so-called debt problem along political North/South lines that are economically and financially unsupportable. Those lines are harmful to the many countries caught up in the North/South rhetoric that have a tangible stake in continued access to private financial markets.

I think it is not a disservice to these countries to say that there is absolutely no prospect for U.S. agreement to a generalized debt rescheduling or moratorium. We will not approach the question on that basis, and I think it is probably best, from the point of view of the interests of the countries that need access to private credit, that this subject be dropped. Reschedulings may become necessary in a few cases. They may not always be what we normally consider to be developing countries; and we will approach this on a case-by-case basis.

NEED FOR INFORMATION

On my third point, we have masses of information, but I think we are still somewhat at sea in our analysis, both because of the gaps in our information about our financial exposure in particular countries and because of the gaps in our knowledge about country debt, overall economic situations, and government policies. A number of the other contributors may point the way for better analysis, both for private lenders and for governments.

Arthur Burns and Henry Wallich have pointed out the need for foreign private and official lenders, for better, more complete, and more widely available information—not only about the size and maturity profile of borrowing countries' external debt positions, but about their economic and financial policies. This is an essential that will be pursued vigorously.

GOVERNMENT POLICY

For government policy, I draw the following conclusions:

We in the government, as well as private lenders, have a problem of information that has to be attacked full-scale. In this, the confidentiality of information must be respected. We must also recognize that a great deal of information about borrowers' positions is not available to public authorities or to private entities and that it needs to be collected.

The North/South framework is not appropriate for dealing with the problems at hand. The developing countries as a whole are not necessarily the problem we are going to face. Financing problems that are potentially more serious are elsewhere, for example, in the Mediterranean and Scandinavian areas. Rescheduling is an action taken in extremes by countries in crisis situations. We have handled these in the past and, despite the higher oil prices, the incidence of major debt problems has fallen off. The questions here are: Is our present apparatus for debt rescheduling, that is, the Paris Club, adequate? Is there room for a greater potential role for the IMF, for example, for recommending a public and/or private stretching-out in the case of major problems (where there is a bunching-up of earlier debt maturities) in the context of the acceptance of IMF conditions in conjunction with a stabilization or adjustment program? Is there a need for another type of mechanism, regardless of organizational framework, for advice on rescheduling before critical difficulties surface?

Incorporating these conclusions, our broad strategy for handling imbalance patterns—which is not a developing country debt strategy as such, but a broader strategy for stability—must continue. Its components are familiar to you: We must work the OPEC surpluses down over time through energy conservation and development of alternative sources of energy. We must encourage OPEC countries to recognize their stake in a healthy world and assume greater responsibility for maintaining its health. We must encourage the financially stronger countries to expand as rapidly as sustainable, consistent with a gradual reduction in inflation, and to accept a weakening of their external positions. We must encourage weak countries to concentrate on stabilizing and restructuring economies to lay a basis for later growth. And finally, we must provide official financing on a conditional basis to encourage this adjustment.

I will conclude on the point that we are in the process of considering a significant increase in IMF resources, which, if agreed, could be of major support on all of the points I have made. We strongly support the IMF's efforts in the areas of financing and in the promotion of needed stabilization and adjustment.

NATURE AND SIZE
OF DEVELOPING COUNTRIES' DEBT
Jo W. Saxe

In analyzing the nature and size of the developing countries' debt, it is useful to make both terms plural. That is, to consider a number of countries which should be taken one by one if the analysis is to be serious. And second, to consider a number of debts, since debts—like countries—are rather diverse. Otherwise, the analysis suffers from aggregation, whether it be geographic or financial.

GEOGRAPHIC PATTERN OF DEBT

Let me first review, very briefly, the geographic side. There are, in current use, a good dozen different universes of developing countries, mostly undefined (and here I'm thinking particularly of what is written in the press where there simply isn't space to define terms). The universes vary from the 1956 universe of almost every country outside of Western Europe, North America, and Japan to the very much smaller universes like the Most Seriously Affected Countries or the Least Developed Countries. I don't need to belabor the point that, for example, Spain is in one universe along with Brazil, and Brazil is in another, smaller universe without Spain. The statistical effects of large countries and the disparate nature of the economic circumstances of the countries in these universes make the aggregates much more misleading than useful. Although I do not deny that for some purposes it is useful to aggregate these countries, it is not useful to do so in talking about their external financial position.

I will briefly commit the sin that I am preaching against because in examining the nature and size of the developing countries' debt, I will deal with an aggregate of sorts. First, however, I will define it, albeit without all the footnotes that one should have.

I am not including the very poor countries, which are more or less self-identifying and which I would describe as countries where the current account deficit is determined by the availability of capital. The balance-of-payments analysis for these countries is rather different from what it is in other countries. These poor countries I would simply describe as does my colleague, Dragoslav Avramovic, who has done some of the best work on this subject, as long-haul cases.

I doubt that, except in specific operations and for very limited purposes, these countries are going to borrow much from the commercial banking system of the industrialized world. The terms on which they do borrow, if they borrow rather than receive grants, are or have become very soft because of repeated re-negotiation of loans, that is, India, Pakistan, Bangladesh, the countries in French-speaking Africa whose debts were simply expunged by an act of the French government in 1971, and so on. There is a concomitant view that aid to these countries should be in the form of grants. This view is openly espoused by the governments of the United Kingdom, Sweden, and a number of other countries. It follows, I think, that it is less and less likely that any very considerable sums of grant or grant-like external finance are going to be available to other less-poor countries on the conventional list of the developing countries.

Although I agree with Charles Kindleberger in his discussion elsewhere in the proceedings that there are going to be some rather serious external financial problems in some of the countries producing petroleum, I will also leave them out of the discussion simply for the sake of convenience and because of my own ignorance of circumstances in those countries and of their external finance. However, the analyst should bear this in mind: Some of the oil producers—let me cite the case of Venezuela to which I have paid a little attention—are countries which both borrow and lend; in this set of circumstances one needs, for analytical purposes, a rather more sophisticated set of accounts than those in common use where there is only one gap which has to be filled to achieve some purpose or other.

The group with which I am dealing is a group which statistically, at least, swamps most of the others. This group is composed of countries that have a fair-sized industrial base which is now growing rather rapidly or has been growing over the past decade or two. There is a relatively modern manufacturing sector and a relatively modern agricultural sector. Most of these countries are deeply involved in international trade. Nevertheless, they do import capital and can be expected to continue to do so over a considerable period in the future. Fifteen or twenty years ago, however, these countries were borrowing from official sources on relatively easy terms. One remembers the AID programs of the United States in the early and mid-1960s. That is no longer the case and is rather unlikely to be the case in much of South and Central America, in eastern Asia, in southern Europe, and in parts of the Middle East. Of course, everything I have said must be prefaced by the statement, "politics aside."

ANALYSIS OF DEBT INFORMATION

Most of the analysts in the field of external debt rely very heavily on the statistical system that is run by the World Bank, called, for convenience sake, the Debtor Reporting System (DRS). It's a very good system. My colleagues have put a lot of effort into improving it, and it is being further improved and expanded. It already provides and will provide, to a considerably increased degree, a fairly faithful record of long-term external liability. What's published is limited to those debts which are public or publicly guaranteed. But also in the system, and being expanded, is the coverage of what is not public or publicly guaranteed in the reporting countries. The countries which report are those which borrow from the World Bank or receive credits from the International Development Association, there are some 100 of them.

One unfortunate thing about the system is that it has concentrated attention on long-term liabilities. I suggested, in the case of Venezuela, that there are some rather difficult problems with our single-entry accounting when the countries involved have assets. Yet, to an increasing extent, the countries about which I am concerned do, in fact, have very considerable external assets. These receive little or no attention if one uses a single system which simply records long-term liabilities.

The liabilities themselves are rather more diverse than they seem. This is another reason for being very, very careful, if not skeptical, in the use of aggregate values. An examination in detail of the circumstances of any one country reveals that there are a good many purposes served by external borrowing. The simple notion that borrowing is equivalent to the current account deficit is manifestly wrong. I'm not introducing a moral note here; I'm just saying that this notion can be disproved by examining the difference between medium- and long-term borrowing and the current account deficit over the past decade for a large sample of countries.

There are a number of corollaries to this proposition which will help with the anlaysis. One is that the countries with which I am concerned are engaged in, or rather their governments or central banks are engaged in, various kinds of intermediation. One important kind is borrowing short-term for working capital and then refinancing at long-term. Let me go back to the dreary statistical detail. If one uses a record of long-term liabilities, and if there is a large increase because short-term debt has been refinanced, then (if one does not know that this is the case) the percentage increase in the long-term debt is apt to be somewhat misleading. Because something that is not in the record has been reduced while something that is in the record has been increased, the conclusion of the analyst who doesn't know that both things have happened will be manifestly off the mark.

In addition, there has been, especially in the 1950s and 1960s, another sort of intermediation—perhaps I am abusing the term slightly—which is the replacement of foreign equity investment with borrowing at interest. This has been in part a matter of expropriating foreigners. It has also happened at the margin because many countries prefer, for one reason or another, to own publicly or nationally the productive facilities in which they are investing. This is important in itself and throws a rather different light on a number of the transactions recorded as an increase in long-term liabilities.

In addition, it has been manifest during 1976 and 1977—although this is a phenomenon that was also happening in the late 1960s and early 1970s—that a number of countries have deliberately borrowed abroad in order to increase their external assets. Again, I'm brought back to the fact that our own statistical system is a record of liabilities; consequently, it must be used in conjunction with other information from other systems.

You are all well aware, I'm sure, that the most reliable estimates that we have of the current account deficit of the non-oil-developing countries in 1976 reveal that the deficit seems to have declined by about 25 percent, from about $38 billion to about $28 billion. At the same time, the external assets of the same countries seem to have increased by $10 to $11 billion. The reasons for this are very complex. The situation of each of these countries is rather different, and I use only the aggregate—despite the criticism I have made of the use of aggregates—for simplicity's sake. Nevertheless, it illustrates the detail into which one must go to understand some of the phenomena which have been, as I have been emphasizing, very considerably oversimplified.

It is particularly difficult to analyze transactions among banks as they are more difficult to classify into the categories to which we are accustomed—because banks are financial intermediaries—than are the transactions of those who borrow in order to invest in the sense of creating fixed capital. An understanding of the relationships among banks requires attention to detail and a wealth of information which lies outside the scope of much of the analysis of this particular set of problems. There is a very interesting effort being made by some of the large New York banks to explain to each other and to interested readers how they classify their assets by nature and degree of risk. The number of categories is large and these categories, I believe, are meaningful from their point of view and also of value to the nonbanker analyst. They do reveal the different sorts of financial and economic purposes which are served by external borrowing.

SIZE OF DEBT

There is now more data around on the size of the developing countries' debt than most people can use conveniently. Moreover, we have no great difficulty in estimating and filling in holes so long as we go at it country by country and add the detail to the total rather than starting with some sort of global view. The data are there (but unfortunately they are a little inaccessible because many of them are on magnetic tapes).

In any event, debts of the developing countries seem to have increased considerably during a period when there was a sharp adverse movement in their terms of trade, in large part but not entirely on account of the price of petroleum. This has now been overtaken by yet other events which have been diverse from country to country. There was perhaps a period of 12 or 18 months when one could clearly distinguish one set of causes and effects. But in various ways these countries have, for the most part, adjusted, well or badly, at whatever cost to their residents or foreign lenders, to a new state of affairs and a new level of absolute and relative prices.

I will not cover the question of the aggregate size of the developing countries' debt in any greater detail, as I hope I have persuaded at least a few people that this is an essentially meaningless concept and number.

In closing, I would submit that the debt analysis done by many of the developing countries for their own use is as good, and their borrowing strategy is as intelligent, as the lending strategy of the more sophisticated and knowledgeable lenders in the industrial countries.

FOR OPEC SURPLUSES
Lawrence B. Krause

Debtors in the aggregate cannot reduce their liabilities unless creditors in the aggregate reduce their assets. This accounting fact of life focuses attention on an aspect of the developing-country indebtedness problem—the OPEC surplus—that has received too little attention in recent public discussions. Unless the aggregate OPEC surplus declines, a fall in the current account deficit of an individual developing country must be matched by an increase in the deficit of some other non-OPEC country. Unless OPEC is willing to reduce its surplus, attempts of non-OPEC countries to reduce their collective current account deficits can lead only to a contraction in the world economy. Furthermore, OPEC countries are not concerned with their current account balances as such; rather, the levels of these balances depend on a number of other factors that have become quite familiar to analysts since the onset of the oil crisis, namely, the willingness and ability of OPEC countries to absorb growing imports, the availability of petroleum from non-OPEC sources, and so on. Thus, it is quite proper to draw attention to the outlook for OPEC surpluses.

How significant one considers the problem of developing-country indebtedness to be depends, in part, on one's views about the short-term (one year) outlook for the OPEC surpluses. While some differences of opinion can exist and some surprises, such as the severity of the weather, can influence the outcome, nevertheless a reasonable magnitude can be determined and an estimate of a possible range can be made.

But the problem is not confined to the short run. The long-run horizon for OPEC surpluses must also be known to complete the analysis of the current situation. For the long run, only conditional projections—guesses rather than estimates—can be made. The range of values that critical variables might reasonably take is so wide that the exercise cannot be undertaken with any precision. Nevertheless, an effort must be made if the analysis is to be completed. The projections also serve as a useful basis for evaluating alternative policy measures, but the degree of uncertainty involved should be not underestimated.

APPROACHES TO ESTIMATING THE OPEC SURPLUS

Two fundamentally different approaches have been used to estimate the elements involved in the OPEC surplus. One essentially extends short-run analysis year by year into the future, making use of all available knowledge, as is done by the OECD in their *World Energy Outlook*. The weakness of this approach is that one's ability to forecast critical variables weakens as the time horizon lengthens. Furthermore, any new influence or adjustment mechanism that may be set off as the process unfolds must be ignored, as must any variable that might come into play after the forecast period but whose existence might be anticipated by the terminal date.

The alternative approach is to begin with a calculation of an equilibrium path for oil prices which can then be used to esti ate the other essential variables in the analysis. The equilibrium price path is calculated by forecasting when in the future the best alternative energy source will become available and at what cost, and then discounting that price to the present by use of the real interest rate. This approach is difficult because we are unable to make exact technological forecasts and the results are sensitive to changes in the real interest rate. (For a discussion of this approach, see William D. Nordhaus's 1973 *Brookings Papers* article, "The Allocation of Energy Resources.")

I propose to combine elements to the two approaches to make projections to 1985. The short-term forecast is made in the traditional way (relying heavily on OECD materials), but rather than just extending the forecast year by year and attempting to deduce real price changes based on supply and demand relationships, three different price paths are simulated. In Case I it is assumed that the real price of oil declines by 3 percent per year through 1980 and then stays unchanged through 1985. The Case II assumption is that the real price of oil remains unchanged throughout the period. In Case III the real price of oil is assumed to increase by 3 percent per year through the period. The price paths have been chosen to correspond to the real rate of interest available on long-term financial assets in the United States, the assumed marginal investment for OPEC surpluses (for simplicity, 3 percent was used on the downside as well as the up). This same real rate of interest was assumed to be earned on net foreign exchange earnings.

The basis for this choice of a price band is the belief that if market pressures were forcing up the price of oil by more than the real rate of interest, it would be profitable for oil producers to cease current production, causing another supply interruption which would lead to an immediate jump to a higher price level. The three price paths can be thought of as corresponding to different degrees of success of U.S. energy policy. In order to convert real prices to current prices, a constant world inflation rate of 6 percent was assumed. The profile of the results is not sensitive to small changes in the inflation rate.

A simulation study such as this is not a long-run forecast. A forecast requires a complete world model, including a mechanism for policy response. Such a model obviously does not exist and may not even be conceptually possible. Rather, the value of a simulation exercise is to point out the implications of a set of sensible values of variables in an interacting system. Simulations often imply a net figure—in our example the OPEC current account balance—which is not intuitively obvious.

THE OPEC SURPLUS: 1973-76

Robert Solow authored the quip, "I never make forecasts about the future, but I am prepared to guess about the past." We need to guess about past OPEC surpluses, since estimates vary a great deal on what they were. Rather than attempting to reconcile the differences, I will merely adopt the figures currently used by the U.S. Treasury (see Table 1). The figures for 1976 are used as the base for projections into the future.

In addition to the jump in oil prices in 1973-74, a couple of significant variables stand out in the evaluation of the OPEC current account results. OPEC imports increased massively, but at a declining rate; starting from a rise of 89 percent in 1974, successive increases were 50 percent and 18 percent in current dollars. (Some estimates place the 1976 increase a few percent higher.) The rise in import volumes, which is corrected for price increases, has been smaller but still impressive. The volume rise in 1976 was probably in the range of 14 to 16 percent.

The OPEC net service balance also is of interest because it shows rising deterioration, despite the fact that OPEC investment income must have been rising. Thus, service imports must have been growing rapidly. This is not so surprising since some service imports are directly related to trade flows and others are tied to domestic development plans. In the projections for future years, investment earnings are separated from other services (which are added to imports to which they are presumably functionally related) with the base figure for investment income for 1976 estimated at $10 billion.

The OPEC current account surplus peaked in 1974 at about $70 billion and declined sharply to $38 billion in 1975 under the combined impact of the world recession, the short-run adjustment to higher oil prices, and the climb of OPEC imports. There was a slight rebound of the surplus to $43 billion in 1976 as the recovery in the world economy led to a revival of oil demand, along with the price increase of October 1975.

TABLE 1

OPEC Balance of Payments, 1973–76
(billions of current dollars)

	Exports (FOB)		Imports (FOB)	Trade Balance	Services,[a] Net	Current Account Balance
	Oil	Non-Oil				
1973	25.2	4.3	20.3	9.2	-4.3	4.9
1974	108.0	6.3	38.4	75.9	-5.5	70.4
1975	97.0	6.1	57.6	45.5	-7.1	38.4
1976	114.7	7.7	67.8	54.6	-11.0	43.6

a Including private transfers.
b Excluding official transfers.
Source: David Maslin, U.S. Treasury, personal communication.

THE SHORT-TERM OUTLOOK: 1977

The most uncertain element in the 1977 outlook arises from the split oil price outcome of the December 1976 OPEC meeting in Qatar. If the OPEC countries resolve their differences and set a unified price (the likely event), then more oil revenue will flow to the high-absorbing OPEC countries, and import growth will be higher. If, however, the breach is not healed, then Saudi Arabia will provide more of the oil for world markets and import volume will be less.

Another element of uncertainty arises because of possible delays in bringing Alaskan oil to market in significant quantities. The Alaskan North Slope and the North Sea (both the British and Norwegian sectors) will be the fastest-growing sources of petroleum over the next few years, with Mexico close behind. The amounts will surely grow rapidly, but the full dimensions are still uncertain.

The most important question about 1977, however, relates to policy actions, or the lack thereof, by the United States. A comprehensive U.S. energy policy would have a profound effect on the world. Though little concrete action could occur in 1977, indeed legislation might take most of the year to enact, the policy proposals themselves could have an impact in 1977 on things like OPEC price setting, because the consequences of the policy could be anticipated. (As of May 1978, the Carter Energy Proposal had not progressed very far, but early indications are that its provisions are not significant enough to justify Case I.) Indeed, it is the various degrees of U.S. policy success that differentiate the simulation Cases I, II, III that follow.

Taking all of the factors together for 1977, the expected OPEC current account surplus is likely to be somewhat less than the 1976 outcome, or about $40 billion. The actual figure should fall in the range of $30 billion to $50 billion.

THE OUTLOOK TO 1985

Case I

Should the Carter administration propose a comprehensive energy policy that has real promise of reducing U.S. need for imported petroleum (technically a shift to the left of the U.S. demand curve for imported oil) and should Congress agree, then the prop will have been removed from world oil prices and they would be expected to erode in real terms. Case I assumes that oil prices decline by 3 percent per year through 1980, corresponding to the period of rapid rise of non-OPEC oil, and then stabilize until 1985 (see Table 2). In response to a declining real price, the demand for OPEC oil rises slowly through 1980 and then more quickly through 1985 (a move downward along the shifted demand curve for OPEC oil). This combination stabilizes the real export earnings of OPEC, but with the low absorbers receiving an increased share, since the volume of exports has increased. Consequently, the rate of volume growth of OPEC imports con-

TABLE 2

Balance-of-Payments Projections for OPEC Countries, Case I
(billion U.S. dollars; 6 percent inflation rate)

Year	Oil Volume (million barrels per day)	Oil Price	Exports	Interest on Foreign Exchange Earnings	Imports	Current Balance
1976	30.1	11.0	121	10	88	43
1977	31.0	11.3	128	14	104	38
1978	32.0	11.7	136	17	121	32
1979	32.9	12.0	144	20	141	23
1980	33.9	12.4	153	22	162	13
1981	36.0	13.1	172	23	182	13
1982	38.1	13.9	194	24	203	15
1983	40.4	14.7	217	25	228	14
1984	42.8	15.6	244	26	255	15
1985	45.4	16.6	274	27	286	15

Rate of volume increase for exports: 1977–80, 3 percent; 1981–85, 6 percent.
Rate of price increase for exports: 1977–80, –3 percent; 1981–85, 0 percent.
Rate of volume increase for imports: 1977, 12 percent; 1978, 11 percent; 1979, 10 percent; 1980, 9 percent; 1981–85, 6 percent.
Rate of price increase for imports: 1977–80, 0 percent; 1981–85, 0 percent.
Source: Compiled by the author.

tinues to decrease and then stabilizes at 6 percent per year. Under this assumption, OPEC's current account surplus dwindles rapidly until 1980 and then reaches a new equilibrium level, which in real terms about equals that achieved in 1973.

The real economic payoff from a very successful U.S. energy policy, however, is not seen in these figures. Rather, it would appear in higher rates of real growth of non-OPEC countries, lower levels of unemployment, declining world inflation rates, and improvement in general in world real welfare. As in other simulation studies, as linear trends are extended far into the future, some unrealistic figures can appear. In this case, the indicated volume of OPEC oil exports in 1985 is 45 million barrels per day; if this high figure were approached, some adjustment would probably be induced, but it is not worth speculating about at this time.

Case II

Under the Case II set of assumptions, U.S. energy policy is successful, but less so than in Case I. As a result, the real price of OPEC oil is stabilized throughout the entire period (see Table 3). OPEC exports hardly rise at all through 1980, but pick up after the big increase in non-OPEC oil is digested in the world market. The rapid rise of OPEC imports still moderates, but more slowly than in Case I, and stabilizes at a higher level of growth since a larger share of earnings goes to the high absorbers.

The OPEC current account surplus under this assumption also reaches equilibrium by 1980, but continues to deteriorate at an increasing rate. Thus, in this simulation, it would be the growing balance-of-payments deficits of OPEC that would set off an adjustment mechanism.

Case III

In Case III, U.S. energy policy is assumed to be only slightly successful. Import demand for oil moderates only very briefly and then resumes its upward (outward) shift (see Table 4). The assumption in this case is that real OPEC oil prices are pushed up by the cartel from the start of the period and continue to rise throughout. As a result of higher real prices, world demand for OPEC oil stagnates until the new non-OPEC oil growth is absorbed and then rises fairly rapidly. OPEC's import growth continues to be rapid, with the rate of growth moderating only slightly.

Under these assumptions, OPEC's current account surplus moderates only very slowly. A new equilibrium could be attained, but only by the end of the period and only if OPEC import growth remains extremely high. It is the nonsustainability of such a high rate of import growth that would probably induce an adjustment in this simulation.

TABLE 3

Balance-of-Payments Projections for OPEC Countries, Case II

Year	Oil Volume (million barrels per day)	Oil Price	Exports	Interest on Foreign Exchange Earnings	Imports	Current Balance
1976	30.1	11.0	121	10	88	43
1977	30.4	11.7	130	14	105	39
1978	30.7	12.4	139	18	124	33
1979	31.1	13.1	148	21	145	24
1980	31.4	13.9	159	23	168	14
1981	32.6	14.7	175	24	191	8
1982	33.9	15.6	193	25	218	0
1983	35.3	16.5	213	25	248	-10
1984	36.7	17.5	235	24	283	-24
1985	38.2	18.6	259	22	323	-42

Rate of volume increase for exports: 1977–80, 1 percent; 1981–85, 4 percent.
Rate of price increase for exports: 1977–80, 0 percent; 1981–85, 0 percent.
Rate of volume increase for imports: 1977, 13 percent; 1978, 12 percent; 1979, 11 percent; 1980, 10 percent; 1981–85, 8 percent.
Rate of price increase for imports: 1977–80, 0 percent; 1981–85, 0 percent.
Source: Compiled by the author.

TABLE 4

Balance-of-Payments Projections for OPEC Countries, Case III
(billion U.S. dollars, 6 percent inflation rate)

Year	Oil Volume (million barrels per day)	Oil Price	Exports	Interest on Foreign Exchange Earnings	Imports	Current Balance
1976	30.1	11.0	121	10	88	43
1977	30.1	12.0	132	14	106	40
1978	30.1	13.1	144	18	126	36
1979	30.1	14.2	157	21	148	30
1980	30.1	15.5	171	24	173	22
1981	31.5	16.9	195	26	201	20
1982	32.9	18.4	222	28	233	17
1983	34.4	20.1	252	30	271	11
1984	35.9	21.9	288	31	314	5
1985	37.6	23.9	327	31	364	-6

Rate of volume increase for exports: 1977–80, 0 percent; 1981–85, 4.5 percent.
Rate of price increase for exports: 1977–80, 3 percent; 1981–85, 3 percent.
Rate of volume increase for imports: 1977, 14 percent; 1978, 13 percent; 1979, 12 percent; 1980, 11 percent; 1981–85, 10 percent.
Rate of price increase for imports: 1977–80, 0 percent; 1981–85, 0 percent.
Source: Compiled by the author.

THE MISSING SIMULATION

There is obviously another policy outcome: the effort to create a U.S. energy policy could fail completely. Such a failure would be perceived as an unwillingness by the United States to confront either the political, the military, or the economic challenge of the OPEC cartel. Under these circumstances, the rate of increase in the real price of oil could probably not be constrained to the level of the real rate of interest and another supply interruption would occur. A discontinuity cannot be simulated, but its economic consequences would be profound in terms of world stagflation and financial disruption.

CONCLUSION

These simulations suggest that the OPEC current account surpluses can be reduced to manageable proportions under a fairly wide set of assumptions. The most important variable may be the growth of OPEC imports about which there is a great deal of uncertainty (see the Appendix to this chapter).

It appears that the world economy will have an opportunity to complete its adjustment to the oil crisis of 1973-74 over the next five years. Such an opportunity is unlikely to appear again for some time. Whether the opportunity is seized or not will be mainly a result of the degree of success of U.S. energy policy. The message is all too clear.

APPENDIX

In order to test the sensitivity of the results to various assumptions concerning the rate of growth of OPEC import volume, a number of simulations were run and summarized in Table 5. All the assumptions of Cases I, II, and III

TABLE 5

Steady-State Rates of Growth of OPEC Imports under Case I, II, and III Assumptions

	Rate of Decline of Import Growth Per Year		
	1 Percent	2 Percent	3 Percent
Case I	D*	6	6
Case II	D*	4	5
Case III	7	8	8

*Indicates growing deficits.
Source: Compiled by the author.

were sustained, except for the rate of import growth which originates at 14 percent in 1977 and which was varied as follows: import growth declined by 1 percent per year (column 1), by 2 percent per year (column 2), and by 3 percent per year (column 3). The numbers reported in the several cells indicate the steady state at which imports must grow in order to reach equilibrium. At a slow rate of decline of 1 percent, the OPEC current account deteriorates throughout the period in Cases I and II. As is seen in the table, the faster the speed of decline, the higher the steady-state growth rate must be. If import growth declines below the steady state, then an expanding surplus results.

PANEL DISCUSSION: PRIVATE BANK
LENDING AND THE DEBT SITUATION
OF THE DEVELOPING COUNTRIES
Richard D. Erb
Robert L. Slighton
David O. Beim
Robert Z. Aliber

Richard D. Erb

Given the subject of the proceedings and the size of the audience attending the conference, a question comes to mind regarding Charles Kindleberger's discussion of past periods of "boom lending" and debt "busts." During the boom periods, what were the perceptions of the risks inherent in such lending activity? What were the judgments of the "pros" including government officials as well as private-sector investors? At the risk of being contradicted by history, let me indicate, however, that I believe that with the improvement in the quantity and quality of world economic information, as well as an increased understanding of economic developments by economists, businessmen, and government officials, the risk of a major, systemwide debt collapse are not very significant today.

One of the central ideas raised in several of the contributions, including Kindleberger's, is the direct relationship between domestic investment and a country's ability to expand its external debt. I think Irving Friedman was correct when he noted that the OPEC surplus is not significant in the way that most people talk about it; there is no direct connection between the OPEC surpluses and the deficits and borrowing requirements of individual countries. I think Henry Wallich was also correct in pointing out that the OPEC surpluses are significant in the sense that they provide an opportunity for other countries to increase their investment. Indeed, I would contend that the deficit countries must increase their domestic investment if they are to continue to run deficits.

The oil price increases resulted in an improvement in the terms of trade of the oil producers and a deterioration in the terms of trade of oil importers. That should have resulted in a reduction in the level of consumption in major oil-importing countries to enable them to export more goods to the oil producers. The surplus-oil countries, however, are postponing their consumption and domestic investment. At some future date, whether in 10 years or 100 years, the surplus-oil countries may want to convert their financial assets into real goods. Alternatively, they may simply live off their interest and dividend income. In either case, there is a need for a higher level of investment outside of the surplus countries in order to generate the income that will service the debt.

Immediately following the oil price increases, many countries borrowed heavily. Unfortunately, they did so not to increase investment but to maintain consumption. Thus, their potential growth in GNP did not keep pace with their growing financial service requirements, and they ran into borrowing problems because banks were reluctant to continue to lend at the same pace. As a consequence, those countries had to adjust their internal economies, and that meant cutting back on both investment and consumption.

The long-term ability of those countries to resume a more rapid growth rate, and thus sustain a higher level of external borrowing, depends on their willingness to increase investment relative to consumption. Thus, the answer to the question that seems to be on everyone's mind—can countries continue to accumulate larger external debts—depends on the degree to which debtor countries increase their domestic capital stock through investment. If not, then eventually the boom in country lending will peter out.

We are all familiar with the financial reporting gaps concerning country debt, but there are more fundamental information gaps that contribute to the difficulties of country economic analysis. We need better information on the ways that countries are spending their money internally. The internal economic data provided by countries do not tell us very much about the breakdown between consumption and investment. In addition, the data usually are provided after a long lag. Nor is there much information about the level and structure of the domestic capital stock for most countries. And yet, it is through additions to the domestic capital stock that a country increases its future output potential and thus its ability to service larger amounts of debt. If country borrowing is to continue to grow, then countries will need to report data on a more complete and systematic basis, including not only financial data, but also domestic economic data. There is much talk about the need for lending institutions to improve their country analysis capability, but country analysis will remain a guessing game until countries report more detailed economic data.

Current problem-country situations have led many to ask what institution will serve as a lender of last resort. I believe we now have—perhaps in contrast to previous periods of financial crises—a number of what I would call lenders of resort. There exists a very complex financial system including not only private-sector loans but also direct government-to-government loans as well as government loans made by official financial institutions. Egypt, Italy, Mexico, and Great Britain are examples of countries which received short-term balance-of-payment loans from other governments as well as from the International Monetary Fund.

Public lenders provide a cushion for the private banking system, thus reducing the risk that a debt problem in one country might snowball into a collapse under the weight of the OPEC surpluses. Today we see similar fears expressed by those who argue that countries cannot continue to accumulate external debt at the same rate that they have over the last two or three years. While that conclusion may be true for some countries, it is not a valid one for the system as a whole. While the accumulation of debt by countries poses some risks, the alternative would be a sharp reduction in economic growth.

Robert L. Slighton

I would like to comment on some of the points made by Charles Kindleberger.

As a banker, I am relieved that he did not include the 1974–76 period along with 1910, 1913, and 1924-28 as periods of mania in foreign lending. There certainly were elements of euphoria in banks' foreign lending during the 1974-75 period.

However, those elements, by and large, are gone now. What remains today is a problem that probably is the opposite of euphoria. Markets exhibit manic-depressive tendencies, and I am somewhat concerned that over the next five years we might enter a period of depressed expectations in which those banks that do not possess substantial analytic capabilities in examining country risk— the large regional banks, particularly—might decide to withdraw from the market and not renew their foreign portfolios as their debts mature.

The decisions of the regional banks tend to be somewhat more volatile because they do not have the capability of examining loans as thoroughly as do the major banks. For that reason, it is highly important that this public discussion of the foreign debt issue be both sober and thoughtful. Because the smaller lenders carry a fairly large portion of the debt, their withdrawal from the market would create severe gaps in financing availability. Thus, the immediate problem is not euphoria at all. If there is a problem, it is a potential depressive swing in market expectations.

There is one significant difference between the current boom market in foreign lending and those of earlier periods. The institutions that are selling debt are retaining a much higher proportion in their own portfolios than was true in earlier periods. This provides a considerable break in the tendency to euphoria.

The suggestion that the IMF and the commercial banking system develop a closer working relationship also warrants comment. The commercial banking system is desirous of cooperating more closely with the IMF than it has in the past. If there is insufficient cooperation, it is not because of an unwillingness of the commercial banks to seek the IMF's point of view but, rather, because of the lack of a convenient mechanism for that contact to be made. I am certain that we will see some such mechanism developed in the near future.

This should not be viewed, however, as a recommendation that the IMF issue might be called a certificate of respectability. That to me implies a binary observation, a yes-no observation, with respect to whether or not a particular country is a good credit risk. Binary observations are not very useful in this area. As a matter of fact, I think they are very dangerous.

In this regard, I would like to underscore Wallich's point on the desirability of shifting to the degree-of-concentration principle in official examinations of the soundness of bank portfolios. Classification of all loans to a particular country is unnecessarily disruptive. It is a meat-axe approach to a problem that deserves sophisticated treatment.

Finally, it does very little good these days for someone associated with commercial banking to say that there will soon be a substantial deficiency in the supply of public international credit. The inevitable tendency is to assume that this is a self-serving observation—that the object is to engineer a bailout for the banks. Nevertheless, I am going to make that observation. I think we are moving into a period in which a lack of public credit will require balance-of-payments adjustments that are unfortunate and unnecessary. There is no doubt that the world is eventually going to have to adjust to the new international prices. Nobody is able to give a satisfactory definition of the optimal pace of adjustment, but it is my opinion that we are very soon going to move into a situation in which the balance-of-payments adjustment is too rapid. This cannot be prevented unless there is some increase in the availability of public international credit.

The problem of insufficient public international credit is more than a developing-country problem. The countries that I worry most about from the point of view of getting their balance of payments under control are not the developing countries but are members of OECD.

David O. Beim

I find Kindleberger's perspective on the developing-country debt question particularly useful. Those of us who work daily with our models and economic statistics of the last few years, or the next few, suffer from a certain myopia. It is useful to have someone lift our sights a bit to see that over the last 200 years the history of international lending has been littered with a substantial number of defaults.

I can't speak of the nineteenth century, but looking to the twentieth century it seems to me that there have been two shocks that were responsible for the large incidence of defaults: World War I and the economic dislocations following it, and the depression of the 1930s. Each of these shocks followed a wave of euphoric lending and was apparently the event that terminated it and turned it to the reverse. I don't see anything in the picture right now that looks to be a shock of that order of magnitude. I don't doubt for a minute that if there were another world war, perish the thought, or if there were another depression, we would be seeing massive defaults on developing-country debts. But I don't think that such events are on the horizon.

What we do have on our hands is a shock of a lesser order of magnitude, but nevertheless a very serious one, namely, the increase in the price of oil. This is not the sort of shock that is likely to cause defaults, but it leads to an increasingly messy situation, which we are having more and more difficulty in accommodating as each year passes. The developing countries have initially tried both to pay for the increased price of oil and also to maintain their rate of economic growth. As Goodman pointed out in the Introduction, it is that desire to keep the rate of growth going, while also paying the higher oil price, that has caused the debts of the developing countries to compound at the rate of about 25 percent in the years 1974 through 1976. This rate of growth of debt is far in excess of any possible growth in the abilities of countries to carry the debt, and the disproportion cannot continue for much longer.

Now one way the rate of growth in debt is reduced is by curtailing development plans. That is something we refer to antiseptically as the "adjustment process" and it sounds very well in the abstract. To the countries concerned, however, it is an exceedingly painful set of events which is often bought at very high internal political and economic cost. I am thinking of the riots in Peru that followed the announcement of the new economic plan, which was apparently a precondition for the loan to Peru last summer; and I am thinking of the riots in Cairo following the IMF's economic plan for Egypt in the early part of this year. I am also wondering what events are yet ahead in Zaire. There are many other instances in which countries that have not succeeded voluntarily in trimming their sails to suit the new events are being increasingly required to do so by banks.

This is the great danger in developing-country lending: not that the developing countries will walk away from the banks, but rather that they will draw the banks too closely into their internal affairs and enmesh them in the political consequences of restrictive policies. This applies to the IMF as well as to the banks. I don't think the IMF will be any more popular than the banks in forcing these adjustments.

Of course, this pressure would ease off greatly if the OPEC surplus would just disappear. I must say I found Lawrence Krause's projections or simulations encouraging, particularly Case II, which assumes that the price of oil does not change and somehow the surplus does go away and turns into a very considerable deficit by 1985. If that were so, many of my concerns would be eased, because the shock I mentioned at the beginning would have gone away.

But it does seem to me there is a limit on the absorptive capacity of the oil-producing countries to take on additional imports and thereby spend their surplus. The limit is their human ability to implement all these projects, something of which bankers are increasingly aware. Many of these countries cannot absorb more imports until they digest the ones they already have.

So I am concerned that the surplus may not go away. If so, someone will be picking up the corresponding deficit. If the deficit does continue to be concentrated in the developing countries, I see politically dangerous and economically depressing consequences. Therefore, I am attracted to the thought that the United States and other strong countries will pick up a significant part of that deficit themselves in order to bring the world more nearly into balance.

Robert Z. Aliber

I would like to suggest some general propositions involving the international indebtedness problem of the developing countries.

The first proposition is that the external debt of the developing countries will not be repaid, in the aggregate, any more than the American Telephone & Telegraph Company debt will be repaid or the Canadian debt will be repaid. The debts of individual countries generally will be repaid as they mature. At the same time, the countries will be borrowing abroad, so, in effect, the funds obtained from the new debt will be used to pay off the maturing debt. Over time, the total external debt might be expected to increase at about the rate commensurate with the increase in national income and wealth, although during some periods the debt will increase more rapidly and in other periods less rapidly.

The second proposition is that the very large increase in the external debt of the developing countries since 1974 has not led to a comparable increase in their debt-service burden because the effective burden of previously contracted external debt fell sharply as a result of the world inflation and the increase in the prices of the developing countries' exports.

The third proposition is that the traditional debt-service ratios (DSRs) have minimal value in predicting when individual developing-country borrowers will not be able to meet their payments on schedule. The major cause of debt reschedulings is that the borrowers pursue excessively inflationary policies, and incur severe balance-of-payments problems, because they are reluctant to permit their currencies to depreciate at rates commensurate with the rates of domestic price increase. The DSRs do not predict domestic inflations. Countries with relatively low DSRs may be unable to make their debt-service payments on schedule if they encounter massive balance-of-payments deficits. And, countries with apparently high DSRs are likely to be able to make their debt-service payments on schedule as long as they avoid bouts of sharp currency overvaluation.

The fourth proposition is that the developing countries have not borrowed enough on a global basis, as judged by comparative rates of return and by comparative rates of growth in national income. The rates of return in the developing countries are substantially higher than those in developed countries, and rates of economic growth in the developing countries are higher than in the developed countries. Both suggest that world income is enhanced by the allocation of capital from the developed to the developing countries.

The fifth proposition is that the rate of increase in the external debt of the developing countries in the last several years has been unusually high, partly because of the oil price increase and partly because of the recession. The developing countries have also borrowed extensively because the funds are there, for the combination of the oil price increase and the world recession meant that the major commercial banks had more depositors than borrowers. There is no significant evidence that the borrowers have misused the funds. Rather, the developing countries are more rapidly approaching the optimal level of external debt. As they near this level, it would be expected that their external debt would grow about as rapidly as their income.

The sixth proposition is that debt reschedulings are an inevitable part of the process because such a large part of the external debt is of such short maturity. Reschedulings, however, are anticipated events, and most lenders are not worse off as a result of reschedulings since the present value of their claims on the developing countries does not decline. Whenever there is a cyclical problem, the lenders become cautious, and, as a consequence, their concern may become self-fulfilling.

The seventh proposition is that most of the estimates of the risk attached to developing-country debt are excessively high. Losses due to reschedulings and defaults do not appear high relative to the difference between the interest-rate markup developed-country lenders get on their loans to the developing countries and the markup they get on loans in the developed countries.

The eighth proposition is that there is no reason to believe—that is, no evidence—that the commercial banks have made any larger mistakes in their loans to the developing countries than in their loans to New York City, Real Estate Investment Trusts (REITS), tankers, and other risky projects.

The ninth proposition is that whether particular loans to the developing countries appear to be used to finance consumption is of less interest than the rate of return on the investments and the rates of interest that are paid on loans to finance the marginal imports. Although it might seem attractive if all loans were used to finance investment, the major concern is whether the individual countries have borrowed too much, not the use of individual credits.

In conclusion, the major determinants of whether the developing countries will be able to meet their debt-service payments on schedule are the stability of the world economy, the growth of their export earnings, and their ability to pursue exchange-rate management policies appropriate to their rates of inflation.

INTERNATIONAL EXPOSURE
AND RISK MANAGEMENT

8

MANAGEMENT OF RISK
Stephen M. Dubrul, Jr.

I would like to review briefly some perceptions that I have from my position as chairman and president of Eximbank (the Export-Import Bank) on the managerial problems involved, not the techniques being used, in lending to the developing countries.

Since 1973 the private international banking system has played an increasingly critical role in financing the non-oil-producing, upper-tier developing countries. This greater role has led to public concern over these banks' ability to perform adequate country credit analysis and portfolio control. Although banker consultations with the international financial institutions can be helpful, each bank must have its own compass to chart the misty waters of international finance. Nowhere is that better recognized than at Eximbank.

Since 1976, techniques of country risk and portfolio analysis have been evolved at Eximbank. The critical element in this effort, however, was to develop, concurrently, a managerial system which permits a logical, organized, and consistent response to the analytical data. Thus, the analysis of credit risk becomes the management of risk, as I'll outline briefly here.

THE CHALLENGE

Today, the only certainty in international finance is growing uncertainty, particularly concerning the non-oil-producing developing countries. The credit position of these countries is well known; the massive deficits, rising debts, and growing dependence on the private banks for financial transfusions have been well publicized. The private banks' role was a key topic among the world's central bankers at Basle in June 1976, and, I'm sure, it will be again this year.

Our impression is that, although several major banks have done good work in country risk analysis, overall the record is spotty. If bank exposure is to continue to rise on a rational basis, much better work needs to be done. Eximbank has had to address the problem because its exposure in developing countries is $17 billion, which represents over two-thirds of its total portfolio—and the share is growing.

Eximbank is an independent agency of the U.S. government whose basic purpose is to facilitate the export of U.S. goods and services through the provision of credits, guarantees, and insurance. Eximbank is self-sustaining; it does not use any taxpayer money or appropriations from Congress. Thus, as is true of private banks, it must grow from its resources—and its wits. Over the last ten years, there has been a dramatic shift in the ratio of credit exposure to the bank's capital and reserves: from 3:1 to 10:1 today. This has raised some questions in government circles about the adequacy of its capital and income available for reserves.

As a fixed-rate, long-term lender, it is imperative that Eximbank have in place risk and portfolio analysis techniques of great predictive quality. The country risk and exposure analyses which we are evolving are discussed elsewhere in this volume. In addition to these analyses of risk, which are undertaken for all countries in which Eximbank has exposure, approximately a dozen countries are singled out for additional supplemental study on the basis of the size of their existing or potential Eximbank exposure. These are, for the most part, countries in the upper tier of the developing countries with ambitious development programs.

Working with the economic authorities in these countries, Eximbank prepares a detailed analog of a cash-flow projection, based on an in-depth study of payments trends and prospects (including details of trade, service payments, and capital flows). We also anlayze the countries' development plans to provide a basis for selectivity among economic sectors and types of projects. This should enable Eximbank to support meaningful projects which are most creditworthy and within its financing capabilities.

While our analysis of risk is oriented toward future lending, it is also used to develop a thorough understanding of Eximbank's present portfolio. This, in turn, may offer lessons which will enable us to avoid mistakes in the future.

Much reliance is necessarily placed upon statistical analysis of the makeup of the portfolio. Eximbank's present exposure and projected exposure, given the existing commitment and repayment schedules, are followed on a comparative basis with respect to the public and private share, the share in each risk category as defined by the country model and the country credit exposure index, and the concentration by country, by geographic area, and by economic sector.

The sensitivity of Eximbank's exposure to possible economic and political dislocations, particularly dislocations that cut across country lines, is also studied. For example, the probability of a sharp drop in copper's price and its possible impact on repayment prospects are considered, both for countries heavily dependent on copper exports and for copper projects in other countries.

Twice each year a major portfolio review is undertaken. The primary focus in portfolio analysis must be to keep management informed, even forewarned, and not caught by surprise in relation to existing or prospective imbalances or problem areas.

The evaluation of Eximbank's portfolio must also be related to its dividend and reserve policy, and to its lending rates and fees. From the ratio of current exposure to capital and reserves, adjusted by the degree of risk perceived in the portfolio, management must derive an appropriate reserve policy. This, in turn, will lead to judgments about the practical rate of growth in exposure and about appropriate future lending margins and fees.

THE MANAGEMENT RESPONSE

The final and key element in the new Eximbank program is to have in place a system which permits a logical, organized, and consistent response to all of these data. Only then has true "management of risk" been born.

Beginning in early 1976, Eximbank underwent a thorough self-analysis. The goals of this analysis were to

State the specific assumptions about the external environment in which Eximbank was expected to operate in 1976-77

Develop a simple, yet comprehensive, statement of the purpose of Eximbank today

Design a clear rationale for each Eximbank program and policy

Test each program and policy against its rationale and the broader statement of purpose of Eximbank.

Establish consistency between programs and policies

The first phase of this review was completed in late 1976, but the process is continuing. The process was akin to an artist reconstructing a subtle-hued Byzantine mosaic or puzzle. We found that policies and programs were intimately interrelated, that changes in one program led to changes in others, and that reviews were required to assure no pieces were missing. We also discovered the importance of the review process itself and the need to institutionalize it. We are now in our 1977-78 review cycle.

Armed with a thorough analysis of present and future risk, a detailed knowledge and understanding of the existing portfolio, and a clearly defined set of objectives which themselves undergo constant review, testing, and anlaysis, a lending institution stands ready to make competent international credit decisions resulting in increased exposure. That's what we call proper management of risk at Eximbank.

9

ONE APPROACH
TO COUNTRY EVALUATION
A. Bruce Brackenridge

As Jerome Blask points out elsewhere in the proceedings, one of the principal reasons for an international bank to evaluate the creditworthiness of a country is to establish exposure limits for individual countries. I would like to outline briefly the procedures which are used at Morgan Guaranty to establish these country exposure limits and to review some of the facts which we use to determine country creditworthiness.

DEFINING COUNTRY EXPOSURE

Both Henry Wallich and Stephen Goodman alluded to the difficulty in defining country exposure. The theory is simple: to distribute the present and potential risk assets of a bank on a country-by-country basis. However, to put this into practice is extremely difficult and involves making many judgments on individual credit transactions. For example, if our Paris office grants a line of credit to the French subsidiary of a U.S. company under the guarantee of the parent, most people would agree that it is U.S. exposure. But what if there is only a keepwell letter? If our Brussels office places a redeposit with the Milan office of Citibank, do we place the exposure in Italy or in the United States? The shipping industry is particularly difficult. We have a client who is the sole owner of a Liberian company which has one asset—a Very Large Cargo Carrier (VLCC) carrying oil between Iran and Japan. In which country does one put this exposure? How are the locally funded assets of a foreign branch to be treated? What about forward and spot foreign exchange? Or Federal Fund lines to the U.S. branch of a British bank? The questions are endless.

Banks have answered these questions differently, as was confirmed by a study recently completed for the Association of Reserve City Bankers. The point

I am making is that, because banks have defined exposure differently, any comparisons of exposure among banks must be viewed with great caution.

The next point is that it is extremely difficult to attain any commonality in the definition and calculation of exposure. The international banks throughout the world have established elaborate and expensive programs to capture the necessary data for exposure reports. We are in the process of improving our computer system for the gathering of exposure data, and our computer people tell us that it will take about ten man-years to design and implement the new system. Since computer systems are so difficult and expensive to change, any attempt to obtain reports based on common definitions of exposure will be extremely costly.

Maximum country exposure limits were first established at Morgan Guaranty in the late 1960s. We calculate our country exposure on what we call the credit-risk basis. Under this concept, each credit facility and risk asset is placed in the country which best reflects the location of the entity having the ultimate legal responsibility for repayment of the obligation. Specifically, this means that the loan from our Paris office to the French subsidiary of a U.S. company under the parent's guarantee is U.S. exposure and, if we get only a nonlegally binding keepwell letter, it is French exposure. We have reviewed every credit facility throughout the bank, including the overseas branches and consolidated affiliates, and each credit facility has been assigned to a specific country. In addition, our system is also able to give us the total amount of exposure maturing beyond one year in each country. We have established limits by country for "maximum country exposure" and "exposure over one year." To my mind, it is exposure over one year which is the most difficult, and we should be concentrating on these figures. Recent history has shown that a bank is able to reduce its short-term exposure when a country gets into trouble.

These limits are reviewed at least annually and more frequently for those countries which are experiencing rapid political or economic changes. Countries like Brazil and Mexico are under almost continual review. Requests for increases or decreases in limits normally originate with the lending officers of the International Banking Division. For countries where we have a significant exposure, such requests are accompanied by the latest country evaluation report prepared by our international economists.

COUNTRY EVALUATION REPORTS

These economists' reports are an integral part of our review of country limits. In determining creditworthiness, our economists concentrate on four specific areas:

1. Policy Factors: A great deal of emphasis is placed on the quality of a country's economic and financial management and whether the economic team is able to make its counsel felt among the country's political leadership. If there

are poor lines of communication between technocrats and politicians or if, for political reasons, a country's leadership feels unable to implement the recommendations of the economic team, then appropriate policies may not be followed, no matter how good the advice of the technocrats.

The promptness of current account adjustment in response to higher oil prices and world recession has been a good test of the quality of the economic teams throughout the world. One of the most encouraging signs for the future is the improvement in the quality of the economic teams of the major borrowing countries. Competent and appropriate policies also assure good relationships with the IMF and the World Bank.

2. Basic Economic Factors: Several points are stressed in assessing a country's underlying economic strengths and weaknesses, beginning with the country's natural resources and the potential for their development. The second most important point is the state of the country's human resources, in particular, the success with which the labor force can be educated and trained for increasingly complex tasks and the entrepreneurial ability of the business group. Third, the growth strategy followed in years past and at present should be in accord with the country's natural and human resource base. If it is not, production inefficiencies may have already occurred that in the future will make it difficult for the country to maintain its international competitiveness, thus requiring increased borrowing or slower economic growth. Fourth, it is important that a developing country be able to finance a significant portion of its investment requirements internally; if it cannot, the foreign borrowing required to support its investment program may result in an overly rapid buildup in external debt. The government should keep its domestic budget under control, while realistic interest-rate policies and other means should be employed to make it attractive for individuals to place their excess savings in financial institutions. Finally, export diversification by commodity and market is important to maintain export earnings in case of price or production drops in one commodity, or recessions in key export markets.

It is worth emphasizing that a particular country's situation with respect to all of these is in large part the result of a process of development over many years and, as such, cannot be expected to change quickly. What is important for the anlaysis is to note whether policies and strategies are in tune with basic factors, or if not in tune, whether policy or strategy changes are likely.

3. External Finances: The policies of the economic team, the basic economic factors, and the international economic situation will all affect the country's external financial position. This position may be described as having four key elements. First, the balance-of-payments outlook should be assessed in detail, with reviews of each of the important trends. Second, the rate at which the country's external debt has been growing and its terms (grace periods, interest rates, and maturity structure) should be analyzed, along with their implications for debt-servicing requirements, and, given the export outlook, the burden of debt service on the balance of payments. Third, the adequacy of the present

level of external official reserves to permit normal trade financing without undue delays and to provide some cushion in the event of export shortfall should be determined. Generally speaking, coverage of three months' import requirements is considered the minimum desirable level, although in single-commodity economies more of a cushion would be preferable. Fourth, although not included in a country's officially reported international reserves, it is important to take note of its borrowing rights in the IMF. These are sometimes referred to as "conditional" or "secondary" reserves in that, in order to borrow, a country may have to make certain commitments to the IMF relating to its economic policies.

4. Political Factors: In assessing political stability, we look for reasonable assurance that, if political change comes, it will be orderly and there will be reasonable continuity in fundamental economic policies. In addition, a country's economic viability must be appraised in the context of the regional and world-wide political situation.

COUNTRY EVALUATION PROCEDURES

Under our standard procedure for the review of existing limits and the setting of new limits, the International Banking Division senior credit officer calls a meeting of the area manager, the lending officers, and the economist who has written the most recent report of the country to be discussed. The presentation gives the economist an opportunity to expand on the salient points of the written report and to discuss his views on future developments in the country. It also permits the other participants to question the economist in detail. Then the territory officers, who travel extensively and who can add their own views on the economic and political situation, review the bank's current position in the country and the strategy for the future.

In these discussions, special emphasis is placed on the mix of the present and planned exposure in a country. Short-term financing is generally considered to be less risky than term loans. Loans to projects with identifiable hard currency cash flows are preferable to those which generate only local currency. A line of credit, which is subject to review from time to time, gives the lender more flexibility than a commitment. In developing countries, exposure to governments and banks is of better quality than exposure to private corporations.

After a thorough discussion of all these considerations, and with an eagle eye on the country-by-country distribution of exposure, the "maximum country exposure limit" and "limit for exposure over one year" are set by the division senior credit officer, who consults with the head of the division on the especially large or sensitive countries. The chairman of the Bank's Credit Policy Committee is kept informed of all changes. In addition, we have reviewed our present limits and strategy for 1977 with the bank's corporate office.

At Morgan Guaranty we are beginning to synchronize the setting of country limits with our forward planning exercises. This process is forcing us to think ahead and answer such questions as: What countries do we see as being attractive for credits over the next ten years? How do we want our credit facilities and risk assets to be distributed in 1980? What measures should we be taking now to achieve this distribution?

One must be encouraged by the progress which has been made in recent years in the quality of country evaluations, which, no doubt, will continue to get better. However, there is a definite need for more accurate, detailed, and timely information. We would welcome the opportunity to work more closely with Eximbank, the IMF, and the World Bank in this area. But more importantly, it is up to us, as lenders, to require additional information directly from the borrowers.

At the end of 1976, Morgan Guaranty had outstanding loans of approximately $1.7 billion to the developing countries. We expect this figure to increase during 1977 and in the years ahead. We follow developments in these countries very closely and have noted that in the past few months economic conditions in several of the larger countries have improved markedly. This is encouraging. However, the commercial banks will have to continue to exercise a great deal of prudence in their international lending. What is needed, from the standpoint of orderly international payments adjustment and a stable financial system, is that banks' lending should neither be so extensive as to allow deficit countries to defer needed adjustment measures, nor be so restrained as to force them into a corner, leading to economic and social collapse.

By nature, a credit officer's work is oriented to the present and the future, but we should also benefit from the perfect vision afforded by hindsight. Elsewhere in the proceedings, Kindleberger refers to a book written in 1951 by Ilse Minsk entitled, *Deterioration in the Quality of Foreign Bonds Issued in the United States, 1920–1930*. This excellent little book makes more interesting points. For those of us who have not been around all that long, we are reminded that there have been defaults by sovereign governments. Also, the author notes that there was a domino effect. After Bolivia suspended payments on its external debt in January 1931, Peru and several other Latin American countries followed in quick order.

I was also fascinated that bankers in the 1920s used almost exactly the same basic factors in determining creditworthiness that are being used by most international lenders today. The defaults of publicly issued bonds which occurred in the early 1930s were not the result of inadequate country-by-country analysis by the bankers, but rather of their assumption that the favorable world economic trends of the early 1920s would continue forever. This faulty judgment led to overexuberance on the part of bankers during the second half of the 1920s and to a substantial number of defaulted bonds in the next decade.

This lesson has applications today. International bankers are now making commitments for loans with final maturities extending out eight years, and we who make credit judgments should be conscious that during this period there may be downturns in world economic activity. Should that occur, the quality of our judgments today will be put to the test.

10

A SURVEY OF COUNTRY
EVALUATION SYSTEMS IN USE

Jerome K. Blask

As has been amply demonstrated, developing-country indebtedness is growing, not only in dollar terms, but also as a controversial issue for bank regulators, politicians, security analysts, and commercial lenders. Among these, it is the commercial lender who has the greatest direct financial stake in the developing world. This is illustrated by the fact that in the largest U.S. banks, developing-country credits now account for as much as 30 percent of total lending.

Consequently, evaluating sovereign credit risk is becoming more and more important. Nevertheless, the procedures that banks follow in making these assessments are not generally known, a situation that prompted Eximbank to survey a broad cross-section of 37 U.S. commercial banks to seek answers to these four questions:

What group within the institution performs the country risk evaluation and with what frequency?

What analytical technique is used in the risk evaluation and does it result in a summary letter or number rating?

Is the ultimate risk assessment tested against actual experience to determine the adequacy and accuracy of the country evaluation system?

What routine uses are made of the "bottom-line" risk evaluation?

I will focus on what the survey uncovered with respect to the last three questions.

ANALYTICAL APPROACHES TO COUNTRY EVALUATION

We began this survey with no strong, preconceived notions as to the procedures followed by U.S. commercial banks in assessing country risk. In fact, our own ignorance about these procedures was a prime motivation for the survey. The results, however, were somewhat surprising.

Four of the 37 banks that participated in our survey, or 11 percent, indicated that they had no systematic procedure for assessing country creditworthiness. In these institutions, political and economic conditions in a particular country were formally reviewed only in connection with the processing of an individual loan request. These four banks have comparatively small international loan portfolios and are relative newcomers to overseas lending. It appears, however, that these four "no-system" banks represent a large number of other U.S. commercial banks. Since our survey report's publication in the *Eximbank Record* and *Euromoney*, several banks have contacted evaluation procedure.

The other 33 banks use approaches to country evaluation that range from the strictly qualitative to those that are more quantitative in character. Three distinct approaches can be identified: the fully qualitative system, the structured qualitative system, and the checklist system. Some banks use more than one system.

Fully Qualitative System

The fully qualitative system is structured around a report that includes a general discussion of a country's economic, political, and social conditions and prospects; the report's format and depth varies widely from country to country and over time.

Five of the 37 survey banks, or 14 percent, follow a fully qualitative approach in evaluating country creditworthiness. It appears, however, that these banks have only recently implemented systematic country evaluation procedures, though three of these banks are experienced foreign lenders.

The fully qualitative system's principal advantage is that it can be adapted to the unique strengths and problems of the country undergoing evaluation. On the other hand, fully qualitative reports tend to be retrospective—a severe limitation on their utility. Moreover, it is difficult to compare readily two or more countries or to construct country rankings on the basis of the evaluations. Thus, it was not surprising to find that only one bank in our survey that used a fully qualitative system summarized its evaluation with a letter rating and that no fully qualitative bank tests its evaluations against experience.

Structured Qualitative System

The important distinction between the structured qualitative system and the fully qualitative one is that the structured qualitative report adheres to a uniform format across countries and is augmented by economic statistics, which may or may not vary across countries and over time. The standard format facilitates cross-country comparisons. The economic data help to provide a basis for deriving a single summary statistic and allow future trends to be projected, thus reducing somewhat the retrospective bias.

The structured qualitative approach was the most popular among the banks surveyed—27 of the 37 survey participants, or 73 percent, employ this system. Of the 27 banks using this approach, 8 summarize the evaluation with a single summary rating; among these banks, the summary rating can take on anywhere from four to ten gradations with five being the most prevalent.

Although the structured qualitative approach, especially when used in conjunction with a summary rating, is conducive to testing the system's assessment of a country against the evaluating institution's actual experience in the country, none of the 27 participating institutions that utilize this system—even the eight that summarize their analyses with categorical or summary ratings—engage in such testing. This is probably one of the more important findings of the survey, and I will consider its implications below.

Checklist System

The most quantitative country evaluation method observed was the checklist, a technique that condenses a country's overall performance into a single letter or number rating. The checklist's rating is derived by scoring the subject country with respect to indicators or variables that can be either quantitative—in which case the scoring requires no personal judgment or even first-hand knowledge of the country being scored—or qualitative—in which case the scoring will require subjective determinations. It is possible to vary the influence that each component variable has on the final score by assigning a weight to each indicator; this is the weighted checklist approach. Conversely, the component variables can be weighted equally, the unweighted checklist approach.

Five survey participants, or 14 percent of the total sample, use the weighted checklist, but only as an auxiliary to another country evaluation system. In four instances the checklist is used in conjunction with the structured qualitative approach. In the one other case, the evaluating institution—in addition to using the checklist—is experimenting with more advanced quantitative techniques.

Because the checklist yields a summary score, that score can easily be correlated statistically against the actual repayment experience of the bank preparing the checklist. Such an exercise could provide valuable insight into the checklist's past accuracy in evaluating country risk. Nevertheless, only one checklist institution engaged in such testing—the only bank of the 37 participating in the survey to test the results from its country evaluation system against its repayment experience.

TESTING OF RATING OR SYSTEM

The finding that the overwhelming majority of survey banks (36 out of 37) do not test their country evaluation system's results against actual experience is an important one. These evaluations are not only time-consuming and costly, but they also have an important impact on many lending decisions—a fact that was confirmed by the survey results. It is important to note in this regard that each of the survey banks with even moderate foreign exposure employs at least one of the three formal analytical approaches to country evaluation that have been discussed.

The survey did find, however, that four survey banks subjected their country assessments to an independent evaluation by another group within or outside of the institution. Although an independent review is not a substitute for testing, it can make the overall evaluation process more rigorous. One survey participant that utilizes such a review procedure actually undertakes three evaluations: an initial country evaluation prepared by the bank's overseas personnel, a review of this initial study by the appropriate geographic division head at the bank's headquarters, and a final review by a special review staff. Two other banks that use a review procedure rely on their staff economists for the review; the other institution submits its country evaluations to an outside consulting group for review.

Given the effort and importance that the survey participants attach to country evaluation, it is somewhat surprising that only one bank tests its evaluations against actual repayment experience. This kind of testing, however, is relatively simple: Evaluations of a specific country over time are compared with the subject country's record in meeting its debt-service obligations. A favorable comparison, or high positive correlation, would tend to verify the validity of the underlying country evaluation system. A low correlation would suggest that the system needs further revision.

Prompted by both the general disinclination toward testing exhibited by the survey participants, as well as the poor results reported by the one survey institution that did test its results against past experience, we decided to test the five survey checklist systems, plus two developed by Eximbank, as to their ability to predict or discriminate between years when multilateral reschedulings occurred and years when they did not. The checklists were used to score 49 countries for as many as 16 years (1960–76), depending on data availability. It was not possible for us to test the fully qualitative or structured qualitative systems—even those with summary ratings—because we did not have access to the ratings.

Before discussing the outcome of this experiment, several limitations should be noted. First, to avoid making arbitrary determinations, it was necessary to exclude the qualitative variables contained in the checklists. On average, only 15 percent of a checklist's variables had to be eliminated. If, in addition, we lacked the weights used by a survey bank in its checklist, then we simply assumed that the checklist was unweighted. Finally, in evaluating the results, it is important to remember that the ability to forecast multilateral reschedulings is only one criterion against which the adequacy of these checklists can be assessed. A checklist bank might find ability to predict the bank's own rescheduling experience or its delinquency and default record a more appropriate standard for judging its checklist's capabilities. Nevertheless, we consider the standard chosen for this exercise to be a good proxy for the checklist banks' own collection experiences because it can be used to evaluate all seven checklist systems on an objective and unbiased basis.

Of the seven checklists, only one was able to discriminate accurately between reschedulings and nonreschedulings. Actually, this checklist successfully predicted 75 percent of the multilateral reschedulings and 77 percent of the non-rescheduling cases. The results using this checklist approach those results achieved by several more rigorous quantitative (nonchecklist) models specifically designed to predict reschedulings. The remaining checklists, however, performed poorly. While predicting 75 percent of the multilateral reschedulings, five of these other checklists were able to forecast, on average, only 45 percent of the nonrescheduling cases. Overall, these five systems were less than 60 percent accurate; the other system's total accuracy rate was a dismal 43 percent.

These results may reflect a weakness in the way the checklist is constructed—namely, that a checklist's component variables and the weights associated with those variables are selected arbitrarily. Some of the nonchecklist quantitative models appearing in the literature have been able to avoid this subjectivity in picking variables and their corresponding weights by using sophisticated mathematical techniques.

This tentative conclusion should not be taken as an attempt to persuade checklist users to switch to rigorous quantitative models which can be time-consuming, expensive, and have their own limitations. On the other hand, checklist users may wish to keep in mind for future versions of their checklist systems what appear to be the major operational differences between the checklists examined during our survey and the quantitative models to which I have been referring; that is, in the quantitative models, as compared with the checklists, there are characteristically fewer variables relating to a country's national income and trade and relatively more variables relating to a country's level and terms of debt.

USES OF THE COUNTRY EVALUATION SYSTEM

The last aspect of the Eximbank survey that I wish to review is the survey findings regarding the use of country evaluation systems in day-to-day decision making. The results indicate that 26 banks, or 70 percent of the survey sample, use their country evaluation results in setting overall country exposure limits. Several of these banks also use the evaluation results to set limits for specific loan maturities and categories. It should be noted, however, that among the survey banks, the country evaluation is not customarily the sole determinant of a particular country's exposure ceiling; marketing objectives, for example, are often another critical factor. Nonetheless, the country evaluation is of considerable importance in setting exposure limits according to the participating institutions that use it for this purpose.

Nine banks that participated in the survey use the results from the country risk evaluation to help analyze portfolio quality; six of these nine also set country limits on the basis of the country evaluation.

The remaining eight banks in the survey sample either do not have a systematic approach to country evaluation or use the system's results in a general way, as a standard for evaluating individual credit applications or to serve as briefing material for senior management.

None of the banks in the survey use the country evaluation results in determining interest rates or fees. Most survey banks view each loan as a distinct product, requiring a unique price determination based on all the factors that contribute to the loan's quality. Interestingly enough, setting insurance and guarantee fees is one of the principal uses for Eximbank's country rating system.

11

A CHECKLIST SYSTEM: THE FIRST STEP IN COUNTRY EVALUATION

James B. Thornblade

In recent years, private commercial banks have become increasingly involved in financing developing countries. As a result, there has been considerable debate concerning the appropriate role commercial banks should play in the development process. I will not address those particular issues but, rather, will outline some analytical tools that provide a basis for more accurately assessing country risk.

DEVELOPING A CHECKLIST

Regardless of the scope of a bank's international activity, it is useful to establish a checklist of economic data to help in determining the risks of international exposure. In all but the five to ten largest banks, the most common decision for the majority of international loan officers in sovereign risk lending is whether or not to take a share of another bank's Eurocurrency credit. This relationship among banks has the disturbing potential for generating "follow-the-leader" behavior. It is healthy to have a diversity of approaches to assessing country risk since that increases the probability that someone, in at least one financial institution, will be able to say in respect to a country and its economic prospects that "the Emperor has no clothes on."

Ideally, every private bank with significant foreign exposure should go through the exercise of establishing its own checklist of economic performance. It would be disturbing if banks were to make decisions on participating in international loans solely on the basis of a country rating which had been bought or "cajoled" from another source, such as a bank, consultant, international institution, or government agency. Although there would seem to be duplication when international officers in different banks search after the same data, there is an important learning process in the individual effort to "nail down the numbers." At our bank, we believe that the area loan officers must, with guidance from the economics department, thoroughly familiarize themselves with the economic conditions in the countries which they present to corporate customers.

Before turning to a discussion of the variables that might be included in a checklist, a few methodological points should be mentioned. First, the variables will generally be drawn from standard international sources. If every international bank had a presence in the major borrowing countries, and national data were comparable, then the checklist could be constructed from a wider range of economic data. In fact, the checklist technique may be helpful for the many banks who do not have a network of international offices and hence must rely on a few international data sources (IMF, World Bank, OECD, and so on).

Second, the emphasis in our work on country ranking has been on analytical, rather than absolute, variables. A few measures of sheer economic size—for example, GNP or total exports—may be useful in a checklist. But in general, the variables that are selected are corrected for size. Thus, the checklist is composed of variables like reserves relative to imports, IMF credit usage relative to fund quota, and so on. The absolute size of the current account deficit is less interesting than the factors influencing that deficit over time, such as export growth and the ability to restrict imports.

Third, there is the question of country coverage in devising an economic checklist for all countries. Very small countries, or nations with significant institutional and political restrictions or with severe data limitations (Comecon countries) should probably not be included. At the other end of the spectrum, major industrialized countries are included in our checklist. While there are some sound arguments in the theory of economic development for *not* including Germany, for example, in the same checklist ranking as Botswana, inclusion of high-income OECD countries sometimes provides a good test of the choice of variables used in assessing debt-servicing risk. There is no reason why these countries should always place high in a ranking. Based solely on economic factors, an "overly mature" creditor nation, like the United Kingdom, may indeed represent a higher debt-servicing risk than well-managed, fast-growing "less developed" countries like Malaysia or Taiwan.

Finally, it should be stressed that a measure of political stability or projected economic performance is not directly included in our checklist. That is why the checklist is intended only as a complement to the country essay, in which the area officer assesses political factors and future events that could significantly alter the performance reflected in the country ranking. Some banks have included the results of a survey of international officers on political and future economic factors in an overall sovereign risk index.

The next section will more closely examine each of the checklist's principal component variables in turn since, taken together, these variables constitute the principal elements in assessing country risk.

THE BASIC PRINCIPLE: EXTERNAL BORROWING FOR PRODUCTIVE PURPOSES

A framework for the checklist is provided by that fundamental principle of economic development which holds that external borrowing should, directly or indirectly, finance projects which increase the borrowing economy's productivity. There can be some external financing of imported gold-plated beds or some balance-of-payments financing (hopefully during a cyclical low in net foreign exchange earnings). Beyond a reasonable point, however, if external debt does not enlarge the productive capacity of a country—and indirectly the export and/or import-saving capacity—debt-servicing problems will arise.

Admittedly, there is no easy way to get a complete assessment of the productivity of investment with the checklist. Nonetheless, a reasonably thorough assessment can be obtained by combining the checklist system—a quantitative approach—with a more impressionistic analysis in a country study which includes the prospects for major projects, the quality of central government and project management, and the outlook for continuity and completion of investments. This broader study would also consider issues of political stability.

The checklist indirectly measures the history of a country's productivity with the variables falling into three groups: measures of level of development, rate of development, and net international liquidity (the tendency to live below the bound of external resources). Generally, a high level of development implies past success in increasing productivity. This means that the economy is probably diversified and the management and education level fairly sophisticated. A high rate of recent economic growth suggests current success in allocating external borrowing for productive purposes. A relatively high level of net international liquidity indicates that the country is already competitive in the world economy; it may also suggest that loans flow into the country in such volume and on such terms (longer maturity, lower interest rates) that the country readily meets its import needs.

Level of Development

It is generally agreed that there is less sovereign risk in, and hence that commercial bank financing is generally more appropriate for, countries at higher levels of development. More advanced economies tend to have more sophisticated management, more diversified and hence more stable production, and greater leeway to restrict consumption and imports in the event of temporary external financial difficulties.

It is not surprising, therefore, that one of the most common variables in a checklist to assess country risk is the per capita income level. The conceptual problems in comparing per capita incomes across countries are too well known to repeat here. The most obvious deficiency is the lack of information on the distribution of income, which the World Bank has estimated for some developing countries but which is not readily available even for industrialized countries. Other broad-based measures of living standards that might indirectly incorporate the effect of income distribution are literacy rate, per capita newspaper readership, and per capita calorie intake.

Other important measures also reflect the level of development and impinge more directly on the balance of payments. A measure of the composition of imports is useful. A higher percentage of imports devoted to food generally reflects a lower level of development, although there are exceptions. More generally, there is the "compressibility of imports" concept introduced by Dragoslav Avramovic in the early 1960s. The structure of exports, such as the share of manufactured products in total exports, is another good indicator of the level of development and also of the stability of export earnings. There are, however, data problems associated with measuring import or export composition, because international trade classifications are still quite unsatisfactory. A recent World Bank study suggests that it is extremely difficult to compare trade categories.

Finally, we add total GNP, which is a function of population size as well as of level of development. It is useful to have at least one measure of absolute economic size because everything else being equal, a larger economy offers more opportunities and provides greater diversity and hence greater stability.

Rate of Development

Indicators of the rate of economic growth are important complements to measures of the level of development. The ideal country risk involves high levels and rates of economic development (Japan, for example). In some cases, debt-servicing risks may materialize in high-income countries with low rates of growth (Denmark and the United Kingdom, for example). In a few instances, the perceived risk of lending to countries at lower levels of development may be relatively low if the country is growing rapidly (Nigeria, for example). As indicated in World Bank President McNamara's Manila address, the difficult risk assessments lie with the group of middle- to upper-income developing countries ($500 to $2,000 per capita income). For this group, indicators of economic growth are an important differentiating factor.

The obvious place to start is with real GNP growth or with growth of real GNP per capita. Again, there are many well-known drawbacks to the use of comparative GNP growth rates and yet, along with per capita income, it is one of the variables most frequently included in a checklist. Another variable that reflects productivity as well as balance-of-payments factors is export growth, which is often closely correlated with GNP growth. In periods of external financing problems, export-led growth is generally to be preferred over growth induced by domestic demand.

We have included the ratio of investment to GNP in the group dealing with economic growth, since it represents a current commitment to future growth. A high rate of investment will generate greater productivity and economic diversification, which assures a more stable environment for debt servicing. In the event of debt-servicing difficulties, countries with ambitious investment programs can also always cut back their programs and thus bring fairly quick relief to the external account. This factor is important in assessing the risk of the relatively high debt-service requirements in investment-oriented countries such as Yugoslavia, Algeria, and Gabon.

A negative factor related to economic growth is the rate of inflation. Rapid growth of real GNP tends to generate a higher inflation rate, as in Brazil and Yugoslavia. Obviously, one would give a lower-risk rating to countries which have achieved rapid growth and experienced only moderate inflation, although lower inflation often reflects price controls or subsidies, which ultimately create distortions in the economy.

We include two variables that impinge on a country's growth via the external trade sector: export price variation and the change in the coverage ratio. Export price variation can be measured by the weighted average standard deviation of export commodity prices for the top three or four commodities in total exports. More simply, one can use the weighted average of the maximum annual price decline of each major commodity. This approach is not valid in the case of countries with a large share of diverse manufactured goods in total exports. An alternative that is valid for both industrialized and developing countries is a measure of the maximum decline experienced recently in the terms of trade (the average of all export prices divided by the average of all import prices). In measuring potential vulnerability to international price fluctuation, we use the maximum relative price decline experienced in any one year out of the last five years or so, rather than the price variation experienced in any one common year. There are still many conceptual problems with these attempts to measure the price variation in traded goods, and it would be worthwhile to refine these measures further. It is significant, for example, that recent debt-servicing problems have arisen in Peru, Chile, Zaire, and Zambia which are all dependent on exports of copper, a commodity with considerable price volatility.

In our current checklist we have also included a variable measuring the change in the coverage ratio (exports divided by imports). An intercountry comparison of this change over a common time period, 1974–75 or 1975–76, is a useful indicator of the ability of a country to adapt to worldwide economic dislocations, such as the oil price boost and the severe economic downturn in industrial countries.

Net International Liquidity

The third and final group of variables on the checklist for country risk deals, directly or indirectly, with the net international liquidity of a country. A large net liquid external asset position may sometimes be an indication of lack of commitment to sustained real growth. It suggests that the government has insufficient planning and vision to convert financial resources into expanded production.

Conversely, it is probable that, in assessing country risk, bankers often feel more comfortable with those developing countries with relatively large net liquid international asset positions. A less-advanced economy is more volatile and prone to inappropriate management decisions, and thus a large cushion of international reserves is useful in carrying the country through a painful balance-of-payments adjustment.

The ideal variable would be one that measures the total net international asset position of a country, with assets and liabilities given diminishing weight with increasing maturity. Thus, short-term external assets count for more than longer-term investments. On the other side in calculating the net position, short-term liabilities weigh more heavily against a country than longer-term debts.

On the asset side, there is the familiar ratio of international reserves to imports, often expressed in months of imports. However, when we use only this measure of assets, we are understating the position of the industrialized countries and some OPEC countries which have accumulated significant nonliquid assets. We use the international reserves data (line 1) found in *International Financial Statistics*, although this data understates the international liquidity of franc-zone countries, which often turn over hard currency earnings to Paris but have significant unspecified access to reserves at the Bank of France. American bankers need a practical and up-to-date study of the access to international reserves by franc-zone countries.

On the liability side, we are currently using two measures. One is the degree of IMF credit drawn by a country. We use the ratio of IMF's holdings of a country's currency to its quota, and, in particular, the broader ratio which includes oil facility and compensatory financing, not just credit tranche drawings. Recently, Christopher McMahon of the Bank of England suggested that a high level of IMF credit usage might actually be viewed favorably, in that it suggests that a country will finally be forced by the IMF process to take tough stabilization measures.

The final variable on our checklist is a measure of debt burden. We use the familiar debt-service ratio (the sum of interest and amortization payments divided by exports of goods and services). Shorter average debt maturity and higher interest rates increase the DSR. This variable is more directly related than any other to the basic question of ability to service debt, yet it correlates poorly with most rankings of overall country risk. The marketplace has given relatively low-risk evaluations (as manifested by lower spreads on Eurocurrency loans) to many countries with high debt-service burdens. The explanation is that the debt burden must be evaluated in the context of the other variables which reflect level of development, rate of growth, and net liquidity.

It can be argued that the DSR is overly complex and says little about future debt servicing. Instead of one ratio, it might be preferable to include in the checklist several debt indicators which are available from World Bank data sheets. To measure the size of debt relative to foreign exchange earning capacity, there is the ratio of total debt outstanding to exports. To determine the maturity schedule and the potential problem of "bunching," one should also include the cumulative debt service over the next five years as a percentage of the debt outstanding.

THE WHOLE IS GREATER THAN THE SUM OF ITS PARTS

As has been continually stressed, there are, for each item on the checklist, problems of measurement, comparability, and even of causal relation to debt-servicing capability. A country ranking based on any one of these variables would be quite unsatisfactory. But we have found that, in combination, the variables on the checklist generate an overall result that makes a reasonable starting point in assessing country risk.

To summarize to this point, our current checklist includes 11 variables.

Level of Development	Rate of Development	Net International Liquidity
Per capita GNP	Real GNP growth	Ratio of reserves to imports
Total GNP	Export growth	Degree of IMF credit drawn
	Investment/GNP	Debt-service ratio
	Inflation rate	
	Export price variation	
	Change in export coverage	

To derive an overall ranking, a country is rated according to its rank on each variable, from 1 to n, "n" being the total number of countries. The rankings on each variable are then added together for a total score which determines the overall position for each country. Each variable in the above list is given equal weight in arriving at the total.

We could not make a strong case for an unequal weighting of variables. The central aspect of country risk is the ability to service debt, which, in turn, depends most directly on factors affecting the balance of payments. Six of the 11 variables—export growth, export price variation, change in export coverage, ratios of reserves to imports, IMF credit usage, and debt-service ratio—are directly related to the balance of payments. Thus, by this selection of variables, we are implicitly weighting the overall results toward balance-of-payments factors.

It was stressed at the beginning of this chapter that a checklist is only a first step in assessing country risk. Why undertake an intercountry comparison of selected data at all? We have found that a country comparison which is relatively free of subjective input stimulates a more incisive debate about country risk and international lending priorities. For example, countries falling in the bottom quarter or third of a ranking might, in an initial review, be held to a zero increase in lending. In order to get an increase in lending for a country which ranks low, the area officer would have to develop a special study, using the checklist variables as part of the framework for discussion.

Banks today are subject to a considerable amount of irrational, as well as rational, criticism of their lending to developing countries. One of the main faults of the less-reasoned criticism is the tendency to lump together all Third World countries based on income level, without regard to the more complex factors affecting risk. In response to criticism, there is much talk in banking about being "selective" in lending to developing countries. A checklist provides a systematic first step in the process of selective international lending.

12

AN EARLY-WARNING MODEL FOR ASSESSING DEVELOPING-COUNTRY RISK

Alice L. Mayo
Anthony G. Barrett

Eximbank has always recognized the importance of systematic country creditworthiness evaluation as an essential part of its decision-making process in the granting of export financing. Previously, these evaluations have taken the form of "structured qualitative" and "checklist" systems which are similar to those described elsewhere in this volume.

During the past year, however, Eximbank has developed a formal econometric approach to evaluate country creditworthiness and to quantify objectively the empirical relationships among economic variables and various measures of debt-servicing difficulty. The structured qualitative and checklist systems and the econometric effort have complemented each other; the result is a three-part country model which provides a systematic and consistent framework in which to make judgments about country risk. The model is reviewed on a periodic basis to reassess the guarantee and insurance fees in the various markets in which Eximbank operates.

Part I of Eximbank's country model, an early-warning model, is the major subject of this chapter and will be discussed in detail. Part II is a quantitative checklist system designed to gauge the medium- and long-range economic vitality of a country. Part III is a qualitative checklist system intended to evaluate the long-range strength and contribution of the country's human and natural resources. The results of each of the three parts are combined to produce a single index for each country which, together with a descriptive country case study, forms the foundation for the country rating.

This chapter was written and presented at the conference by Alice L. Mayo, but it is the result of their joint research.

EXIMBANK MODEL: PARTS II AND III

Part II of Eximbank's country model is designed to simulate the mental process of the country economists in their assessment and weighting of the key economic variables which influence a country's economic posture over the medium and long term. The economic variables included and their respective weights were chosen by the country economists; ten key variables were selected as most representative of a country's economic health. These ten variables, weighted unequally, were grouped into four major categories: wealth, as measured by GNP per capita; magnitude and efficiency of capital investment, as measured by the capital-output ratio and level of investment; fiscal and monetary policy, as indicated by the rate of inflation and government deficit or surplus; and magnitude and vulnerability of foreign exchange earnings, as measured by current account performance and export commodity dependence. Each of the major categories contains several variations of these measures.

Part III of Eximbank's country model emphasizes the nonquantifiable human and natural resources that are significant over the longer term. As with Part II, it also includes ten variables selected by the country economists. They are grouped as follows: management competence and policy; infrastructure and stage of economic development; attitude and responsibility as indicated by work ethic and repayment experience with Eximbank and others; and physical resources and economic self-sufficiency. All of the variables are assigned equal weight. Part III is the most subjective of the three parts of the country model; to minimize bias, however, and to ensure consistency of scoring, each country's rating for each variable is agreed to by a consensus of the country economists.

DEVELOPMENT OF PART I: AN EARLY-WARNING MODEL

As with any econometric analysis, the early-warning model is based on the principle that there is a measurable historical relationship among a set of explanatory economic indicators on the one hand and a dependent "explained" variable on the other, which can be identified through statistical or econometric tests and can be used to predict the dependent variable. The specific model presented here is an application of this principle, using economic data for a number of countries to explain debt-servicing difficulty.

Genesis of the Early Warning Model

Given the wide acceptance of this basic principle in the physical and social sciences, and the development in recent years of numerical credit-scoring models based on this principle for bond and consumer credit ratings, it is somewhat surprising to find only three major studies which rigorously attempt to apply this principle to the problem of assessing country credit risk. The three are: a study by Charles Frank, Jr., and William Cline in 1971, one by Earl Grinols in 1975, and a recent study by Gershon Feder and Richard Just.

The purpose of the Frank and Cline paper—the seminal study in this field—was to predict whether or not a country would formally reschedule its external debt. The study was based on a data sample for 26 countries over a ten-year period, 1960-69. Twenty-one instances of formal multilateral reschedulings were included.

Using discriminant analysis, an econometric technique similar in the linear case to ordinary least-squares regression, Frank and Cline principally concluded that three short-term variables were significant in determining whether or not a country rescheduled its debt: the traditional debt-service ratio (the ratio of debt principal and interest payments to exports), the ratio of debt amortization to total debt outstanding, and the ratio of imports to international reserves.

The Grinols study builds upon the Frank and Cline study using the same technique with, however, somewhat different variables. Additionally, some necessary data adjustments were made which were not recognized in the earlier work. Overall, however, the Grinols study does not add significantly to the state of the art.

A more recent study by Feder and Just also uses the Frank and Cline work as a foundation, using the same variables but adding several new ones. Feder and Just, however, criticize the previous work on statistical grounds, particularly the use of discriminant analysis. The principal flaw in using discriminant analysis for this type of "yes" or "no" problem is the violation of the important normality assumption. To correct for the statistical deficiencies of discriminant analysis, Feder and Just use logit analysis, an econometric technique specifically designed to deal with categorical qualitative dependent variables such as whether or not a country reschedules its debt.

Using logit analysis and nine economic indicators, of which seven were also considered by Frank and Cline, for the time period 1965-72, the two authors found twice as many significant explanatory variables for the 21 instances of rescheduling. The variables include the debt-service ratio, the ratio of debt amortization to total debt outstanding, the ratio of imports to international reserves, income per capita, the ratio of capital inflows to debt-service payments, GDP growth, and export growth. Furthermore, they had a lower rate of error, between 12 and 26 errors with 145 observations in the previous study. Feder and Just, unlike Frank and Cline, include medium- and long-term, as well as short-term, economic variables.

Eximbank's early-warning model builds upon the works of Frank and Cline and Feder and Just but extends the application of logit analysis by enlarging the sample to include more countries and a longer time period; examining additional economic variables; looking at alternative measures of debt-servicing difficulty in addition to formal multilateral reschedulings, such as Eximbank reschedulings and claims; and making the model forward-looking. That is, the model is intended to predict different types of debt-servicing difficulty up to five years in advance, thereby obviating the need to project or to lag the explanatory variables as was done in the two previous works.

Description of the Data Base

Before presenting the results of the model, it may be useful to describe the data base for those who are interested in identifying additional data sources. The core data include about 50 basic variables for 48 countries for the period 1960–75, with debt projections extending to 1980. The data base includes approximately 40,000 observations. The total debt outstanding of the 48 countries in the sample accounted for 93 percent of the total debt outstanding of all developing countries in 1975.

The IMF's *International Financial Statistics*—probably the most important single data source—provided data on the national income accounts, including gross domestic product, government revenue and expenditures, and fixed capital formation; money supply; domestic credit; reserve position in the IMF; international reserves; exchange rates; consumer prices; population; and balance of payments, including exports, imports, largest export, current account balance, and short-term capital flows.

The World Bank's *Debt Tables* provided the basic debt data, including disbursed and total debt outstanding, commitments, principal and interest payments, and supplier credit and private bank disbursed and total debt outstanding. The United Nations' *Yearbook of International Trade Statistics* provided data on net oil imports and essential imports. The Bureau of Mines' *International Petroleum Annual* served as a second major source of net oil import data. The rescheduling data were provided by the World Bank, the U.S. Treasury Department, and the U.S. State Department.

Data for nine variables relating to different measures of debt-servicing difficulty were generated by Eximbank, including political and commercial claims, loan payments delinquent 90 days or more, and Eximbank reschedulings, all by type of credit: government, private with government guarantee, and private nongovernment guaranteed. Eximbank also provided data on exposure and country ratings.

From the 50 basic variables, a myriad of groupings and ratios were formed. The number of variables was then reduced to a more manageable level based on an analysis of simple correlation coefficients, principal components, and results of pretests of the logit model.

RESULTS USING THE EARLY WARNING MODEL

The results obtained with the early warning model using one measure of debt-servicing difficulty, that of formal multilateral reschedulings, are the most useful to review for continuity of discussion and for comparison with the earlier studies.

The dependent variable is binary, that is, it indicates whether or not a formal multilateral rescheduling occurs. However, in a departure from the previous studies, the occurrence of rescheduling was redefined to include a rescheduling up to five years hence. Thus, the dependent variable may take on one of two values depending on whether: a rescheduling will occur sometime within five years, meaning either in the current year or anytime up to five years hence; or no rescheduling will occur within five years. (A period of five years was chosen to reflect the normal maximum term of commercial bank lending.)

The sample for this logit model included 571 observations for 48 countries, almost 2.5 times the number of observations in the Feder and Just study and approximately 4 times the number in the Frank and Cline study. The sample covered 28 instances of formal multilateral reschedulings in 11 countries.

The six variables used in the final reestimated logit model are the ratio of disbursed debt outstanding to exports, the ratio of international reserves to imports, the ratio of gross fixed capital formation to GDP, the ratio of imports to GDP, the ratio of reserve position in the IMF to imports, and the rate of increase in consumer prices.

These six variables were chosen on the basis of several statistical criteria: correctness of the sign of the coefficient, consistency of the sign of the coefficient over a number of alternative logit estimations, stability and significance of the t-statistics (a measure of predictive significance), and the change in the predictive capability of the equation when the variable was dropped from the model either by itself or as one of a group of variables.

The signs (or direction) of the coefficients of the variables in the model appear correct. As the ratio of disbursed debt outstanding to exports increases, the more likely the country will be a candidate for rescheduling and the variable has the appropriate positive sign. Both the ratio of international reserves to imports and the ratio of the reserve position in the IMF to imports have negative signs, indicating the stronger the reserve position, the less likely a rescheduling will occur. The ratio of gross fixed capital formation to GDP also is negative, as expected; as a country devotes more of its resources to long-term investment, it increases its productive capacity and strengthens the economy, thereby decreasing the likelihood of rescheduling. The rate of increase in the consumer price index represents the domestic inflation rate, and the higher this rate, the more likely the country is going to experience debt-servicing difficulties.

At first, it would appear that the negative sign for the ratio of imports to GDP is inaccurate. However, this ratio can be viewed as a proxy for the degree of "openness" or maturity of the economy, and the more open or mature the economy, the less likely it is to reschedule. (The ratio of exports to GDP can be substituted in the model for the import to GDP ratio with little loss in predictive capability.)

Despite the importance they played in both the Frank and Cline and Feder and Just studies, the debt-service variables were dropped because of their poor statistical performance and mixed results over a large number of estimations.

The historical data on debt service relate to principal and interest payments actually made. In the case of a rescheduling, however, the principal and interest payments made would be substantially less than those that would be due in the absence of the rescheduling, and which prompted the rescheduling in the first place. To circumvent this difficulty, Frank and Cline and Feder and Just both substituted a hypothetical debt service for the actual debt service in those countries and years in which there were reschedulings. The necessary data adjustment could, however, seriously bias the model results.

All of the t-statistics for the six variables included in the model are strongly significant at a 5 percent confidence level. The detailed results of the model are presented in Table 6.

TABLE 6

Logit Parameters for Probability of Rescheduling

	Coefficient	t-Statistic
Ratio of disbursed debt outstanding to exports	0.876	5.015
Ratio of international reserves to imports	-3.520	-4.047
Ratio of imports to GDP	-9.215	-3.737
Ratio of reserve position in IMF to imports	-6.340	-3.158
Ratio of gross fixed capital formation to GDP	-5.259	-2.510
Percentage change in consumer price index	1.500	2.090
Constant	0.090	0.133

Log-likelihood ratio = 147.172.
Log-likelihood ratio index = 0.63.
Note: Probability of rescheduling = exp [0.090 + Z]/1 + exp [0.090 + Z] where: exp denotes exponential and Z is the sum of the product of the coefficients and parameter values (Z = sum $b_i X_i$) where the b_i's are the above coefficients and the I_x's are the values for the six variables.
Source: Compiled by the authors.

In assessing the predictive power of the model, a prediction of rescheduling was judged to be accurate if the country actually rescheduled anytime within five years of the prediction and was judged to be inaccurate if there was no rescheduling during the period. Using a probability cutoff selected to equalize the share of errors in each category, the model was able to predict correctly a rescheduling up to five years in advance in 76 percent of the cases. A prediction of no rescheduling was judged to be accurate if the country actually did not reschedule anytime within five years of the prediction and was judged to be inaccurate if there was a rescheduling during the period. In 87 percent of the cases, the model correctly predicted that a rescheduling would not occur. The log-likelihood ratio index, somewhat equivalent to the coefficient of determination or R^2 in ordinary least-squares regression, is .63, indicating that the early-warning model can predict for the period up to five years in advance of a rescheduling with an overall rate of accuracy of about 63 percent.

It is not possible to compare the results of the Eximbank early-warning model directly with the Frank and Cline and Feder and Just results which relate only to predictions of rescheduling in the current year; the early-warning model, as has been indicated, extends the predictive power to a time horizon of five years.

CONCLUSIONS

We hope that the current quantitative effort at Eximbank, and similar efforts now underway, to develop techniques to assess better developing-country risk will help to broaden the horizons for the application of available techniques to assess the repayment prospects of countries. Application of these techniques and their results have implications not only for international financial lenders in assessing country creditworthiness but for international borrowers as well in assessing their own credit-risk posture and debt-servicing capacity.

The three-part Eximbank country model has been of considerable interest to the associates at Eximbank. The overall country model presents a comprehensive picture of many of the factors which are relevant to creditworthiness evaluation. By integrating econometric analysis with more traditional analysis, we are better able to make systematic and consistent judgments and to refine our process of thinking as the future becomes history.

13

WORLD BANK TECHNIQUES
FOR COUNTRY EVALUATION

John A. Holsen

The World Bank Group has no set formula for creditworthiness analysis. As we gain experience and face new situations, we have to modify our techniques and procedures. This has been especially true in the last few years—during which borrowing from private financial institutions has grown so rapidly. Like you, we are continuously trying to improve our methods of country evaluation.

CATEGORIES OF BORROWERS

In the fiscal year which ended June 30, 1976, the World Bank Group approved 214 long-term loans to 77 different countries for a total of $6.6 billion. These figures combine two very different kinds of financing. Twenty-six countries received International Development Association (IDA) credits only. These credits are provided on highly concessional terms almost entirely from funds given us by governments. Thirty-eight countries received only World Bank loans. These loans are on quasi-commercial terms and are made principally from resources which we obtain from the sale of bonds in the capital markets of the industrial and the major oil-exporting countries. Another 13 countries were what we call "blend" countries—they received a mixture of Bank and IDA financing.

This already suggests at least three broad classes of countries from the point of view of creditworthiness: those we consider not currently creditworthy for regular World Bank loans but which are eligible for "soft" IDA credits; those which we consider fully creditworthy for the approved amount of "hard" Bank lending; and those with limited creditworthiness for Bank financing, which consequently receive varying blends of "hard" and "soft" resources. There are, exceptionally, also a few countries which are creditworthy for Bank lending, but to which we provide IDA credits (alone or in a blend with Bank resources) simply on the grounds of their poverty. The two other categories are those countries where either economic performance or project preparation is insufficient to justify any financing on either hard or soft terms, and those countries that are sufficiently well established in the capital markets that they no longer require financing from the World Bank Group.

The countries no doubt of greatest interest to you are those that we consider creditworthy for Bank loans; that is, loans on quasi-commercial terms. During 1977, the Bank's terms are 8.2 percent interest, with final maturities generally of 15 to 22 years, including grace periods normally of three to four and one-half years. In our loans, the interest rate is fixed for the life of the loan but is related to our own average costs of borrowing during the year prior to the issuance of the loan. Last year, three-fourths of the Bank Group's lending—about $5.0 out of $6.6 billion—was on Bank terms. This high proportion of hard lending is partly because concessional IDA resources are limited in amount, and partly because concessional IDA resources are limited in amount, and partly because most of the major borrowers among the developing countries are considered creditworthy.

World Bank loans are made only to, or with the guarantee of, governments; consequently, our evaluation procedures concentrate on overall country creditworthiness.

Governments may default on loans either because government revenues are inadequate or because they lack, due to balance-of-payments problems, the foreign exchange to make the required payments. One and usually both of these factors are common in the poorer developing countries, which explains why they generally are not considered creditworthy for World Bank loans. The fact that the financed projects offer good economic rates of return does not mean that it is easy for the governments concerned to capture enough of the benefits to cover debt service. This is particularly the case when the project concerned is for economic or social infrastructure, not offering a direct financial return (such as roads or schools). In such cases, debt service must be paid from general government revenues. It is not difficult to imagine the problems that governments have in mobilizing financial resources when per capita incomes are on the order of $100 and $200 per year.

Since the middle-income developing countries are economically much stronger, they are consequently the main clients for World Bank loans, just as they are for loans from private financial institutions. Experience indicates, however, that some of them will, from time to time, encounter periods of external financial instability which may become sufficiently severe that debt rescheduling becomes necessary. These episodes may have their origin in adverse external trends, in seriously inadequate internal economic management, or, more likely, in one aggravated by the other.

While internal financial instability will usually have its proximate cause in inadequate fiscal, monetary, and incomes policies, we also look at economic management in the broadest sense. By this we mean the effectiveness with which public policy and public and private resources and capacities are being, and can be expected to be, directed toward the promotion of economic growth. In the short run, one may think of economic growth mainly in terms of expanding output, but over the longer run it is also essential that the benefits of growth be shared in a socially accepted manner.

FACTORS CONSIDERED IN THE COUNTRY EVALUATION

If we put aside the countries which are not considered creditworthy for Bank lending, mainly because of their relative poverty, the task of country evaluation in the Bank Group centers mainly upon four areas.

First, as has been indicated, we analyze the quality of the country's financial and economic management. The extent to which the public sector's investment expenditures are financed by public sector savings is a major concern; some domestic borrowing is normally appropriate, but it should be from noninflationary sources and should not unduly restrict credit available to the rest of the economy. We find ourselves concerned with what we call "keeping the prices right." This covers such things as real interest rates offered savers and charged borrowers, the exchange rate, income policies, and the prices or tariffs charged by public-sector enterprises. As the time horizon expands, factors such as the provision of adequate social and economic infrastructure, the promotion of nontraditional exports, and attention to depressed or backward regions get relatively more attention. For countries with substantial external debt we have been increasingly concerned about the borrower's own debt management policies, that is, whether they are implementing programs to keep external borrowing within reasonable limits, to negotiate the most favorable terms that are available, and to allocate their borrowing capacity to priority purposes. The effectiveness of the country's capital markets in mobilizing and allocating financial savings is another important topic. In practice, the policy areas upon which we concentrate vary, depending on what we judge to be most significant in the particular case.

Second, we look at the impact of expected trends in the world economy upon the country being evaluated, especially via changes in the demand for its exports and the availability of external capital from other official and private sources.

Third, we look at the public debt and public debt-service burden which has been inherited from the past. To the extent data permit, we look at all of a country's external assets and liabilities.

Finally, a judgment must be made on the country's capacity to adjust in the face of unknown future developments. Oil prices will rise, droughts will come, and export prices will fluctuate in ways and at times we cannot expect to predict. The only thing we can be certain of is that the scenarios in our carefully worked-out economic projections will be wrong in some important respects. What then becomes important is the ability of a country to adjust to these unknown future events. This has to be judged on the basis of its economic structure, its record of economic management in past periods of difficulty, its international reserves, and how its own reserves can be supplemented by adjustment assistance that can be mobilized from abroad.

PROCEDURES FOR COUNTRY EVALUATION

The necessary country studies are the responsibility of the country economists assigned to our operating departments. For example, in the Latin American region we have 31 country and senior economists whose primary assignment is the continuing analysis of the economic position and prospects of the borrowers in the region. They are aided by their colleagues in the central economic staff who are concerned with medium- and long-term trends in commodity markets, who maintain the Bank's Debtor Reporting System, who study trends in international financial markets and in the industrial countries, and provide numerous other forms of support for our country analyses. The country economists—usually generalists—are also able to call upon a wide variety of specialists when it comes to analyzing the problems of specific sectors. Moreover, they benefit from the Bank's close cooperation with the IMF.

In addition to the country economic work done in the operating departments, a group in the Office of the Vice President for Finance, known as the Loan Portfolio Analysis Unit, also contributes to the overall analytical effort. This group is concerned more with the Bank's total risk exposure than with the creditworthiness of individual borrowers, although it does form its own independent view on the latter. The Bank monitors its loan portfolio as a whole to ensure that the distribution by risk categories is kept within prudent limits. Other important aspects of the country evaluation process include the limits on both the share of our loans going to any one borrowing country and the share of any country's debt and debt service which is due the Bank. In the latter case, however, there is some flexibility in the sense that we are willing to accept somewhat larger shares when the totals themselves are relatively small. Nevertheless, these considerations of general portfolio management may restrict lending in cases where country considerations alone would indicate creditworthiness for higher levels of Bank lending.

INDICATORS OF CREDITWORTHINESS

So far, I have not suggested specific analytical techniques. This reflects our experience that there is no adequate checklist or formula which takes into account all the relevant variables; such techniques can be no more than starting points for country evaluation. We do, however, use quantitative indicators insofar as this is practical.

One measure we and others use widely is the common debt-service ratio: the ratio of interest and amortization payments to export earnings. But there are hazards in even this seemingly simple ratio. The same ratio means very different things in different countries. A ratio of 20 to 25 percent for a small country where exports are large relative to the total economy would probably be cause for concern, while the same DSR would be very easily managed in a country such as Brazil or Mexico. Moreover, the significance of a particular ratio, even in the same country, changes over time. For example, in recent years the increase in the conventionally calculated DSR has overstated the increase in the effective debt management burden in many middle-income developing countries, because of the changing composition of their debt.

There is a great deal of difference between obtaining project loans from the World Bank and borrowing in the Eurodollar market. The World Bank loan normally requires several years of project preparation and then the loan is likely to be disbursed over the following three to six years; the Eurodollar credits can be negotiated and disbursed quickly as long as creditors take a favorable view of the borrower's financial management and prospects. As credits from financial institutions, not linked either to particular imports or to progress in project implementation, have become a larger share of debt and debt service, it has become correspondingly easier for borrowers to mobilize new resources which, in effect, offset amortization payments on previous borrowing with comparatively short original maturities. In these circumstances, we are giving increasing attention to the interest burden and relatively less to the total DSR.

The best all-around quantitative creditworthiness indicators to be found in the balance-of-payments data are probably the trends, both historical and pro-jected, in exports, imports, the trade deficit, and the current account deficit. At the present time, after many developing countries have been borrowing to finance balance-of-payments deficits which were clearly larger (in relation to GNP and exports) than could be sustained, the crucial question is whether or not these countries are making the necessary adjustments to reduce their trade deficits and hence their current account balance-of-payments deficits to levels which can be sustained over the longer run. The simple fact that a deficit exists, of course, does not signify a problem; a continued capital inflow, which is what the deficit indicates, is beneficial for both the lender and the borrower when the resources are well used and the returns on investment are comparatively high.

When one looks at projections of exports and imports, it is also necessary to consider the possible variations in these estimates. To what extent do export earnings depend upon relatively few products and markets? Are export earnings therefore subject to wide fluctuations? If export earnings are particularly un-certain, can imports be substantially reduced without serious injury to the economy? Are the country's international reserves adequate to offset likely short-term variations in export earnings? I do not want to overemphasize this set of questions, however. Our own analysis suggests that the long-term growth rate in export earnings is considerably more important than possible year-to-year fluctuations in export receipts. Thus, we concentrate more on the prospects of expanding exports (which in practice usually means the growth of nontraditional exports) than upon possible year-to-year fluctuations in export earnings. The strengthening of international arrangements such as the IMF's Compensatory Finance Facility further reduces the risk from cyclical fluctuations in export earnings.

Problems of external financial instability often are the result of internal financial instability which sooner or later "spills over" into the balance of payments via lagging exports and a rapid growth in import demand. Consequently, one can often anticipate external financial problems by looking at the financial management of the public sector. The indicator we most widely use in this regard is the public-sector deficit as a percentage of gross domestic product (GDP). Public-sector savings in relation to GDP, and to investment expenditures, are important related indicators. Here again, it may be possible to anticipate trends by looking at the public sector's anticipated investment expenditures and their likely financing. Ambitious expenditure programs unmatched by increases in revenues and public-sector savings are almost certain to result in problems.

WORLD BANK ROLE

The World Bank has been concerned not only with measuring and forecasting but also with exercising a constructive influence on events. In some cases this involves helping countries to prepare medium-term programs for public-sector investments and their financing; in other cases we review the government's programs and offer our suggestions. In our own lending operations we are likely to have "project conditions" that will strengthen public-sector resource mobilization; the most common examples concern the tariffs charged by public enterprises. Thus, we are concerned with improving as well as measuring creditworthiness.

My review of the World Bank's approach to creditworthiness analysis has been a quick summary of a complex subject. If I seem to have placed emphasis upon the general economic management of the borrowing countries rather than upon specific analytical techniques and tools, that is because I intended to do so. We have found no substitute for an informed judgment based upon a careful analysis of the economic condition and prospects of the borrower.

CHAPTER

14

PANEL DISCUSSION: MANAGING AND
ASSESSING DEVELOPING-COUNTRY RISK
Stephen D. Eccles
Roman Senkiw
William R. Cline
Carlos T. DeArrigunga

Stephen D. Eccles

The area that I will focus my comments on has been mentioned elsewhere in this volume, but it has also arisen in most of the conversations I have had recently with the major commercial banks heavily involved in developing-country lending, that is, the question of information and data. I would like to make a few remarks and pose a few, perhaps leading, questions to the banks on this subject.

I would be the first to agree that the data base for creditworthiness analysis used by commercial lenders is generally not good. Perhaps the major area for improvement in creditworthiness analysis today is not in the methodology, but rather in the data base.

It has often been said that the World Bank and the IMF have a lot of confidential data; if only they would give it out, everyone would be a little bit better off. One ought to ask, If the Bank and the IMF do have all this data, why do they get it? I cannot talk for the IMF, but the Bank obtains the data it has, not because of any special legal right, but simply because we insist upon having it. We have no more ways of obliging anybody to give us any data on any subject at all than do other lenders. If you lend, you have a reasonable basis for requesting relevant information; this is as true for the commercial banks as it is for the World Bank. However, it may be the case that we have easier access because many borrowers appreciate the anlaysis we give to this data, which enables us to have a positive dialogue with the countries about economic policies.

The Bank devotes a good deal of time to information collection and analysis because we feel that, for a proper understanding of the creditworthiness of a country, you have to dig rather deep. As John Holsen comments elsewhere in the proceedings, in his region alone (Latin America and the Caribbean), we have 31 economists who are backed up by central staffs doing such work as commodity analysis. We are dealing in numbers of economists per country, whereas commercial banks usually talk of the number of countries per economist—often tens and twenties of countries per economist.

If one is so thin on the ground, it is very difficult to assess the creditworthiness of countries, for it takes much more than just analyzing raw data. One has to have a feeling for the quality of the management of the economy above all else, and I know of no way that can be obtained, except very superficially, from an analysis of data. You have to know the country; you have to know what makes it tick—very much along the lines of the comments made by Bruce Brackenridge. If you ask enough questions, go there enough, talk to the policy makers enough, you come away with some sort of feel as to whether that country is well managed or not.

This judgment about management is essential because no lender, whether the World Bank or a commercial bank, is ever the only lender. For example, although we make quite sophisticated projections as part of our creditworthiness analysis, these have to include assumptions about taking on debt from sources over which we have no control. Thus, our own creditworthiness assessment is heavily reliant upon the assumption that the borrowing country will not borrow indiscriminately from other sources. I think a major factor in distinguishing a good risk from a bad risk, apart from whether the country has a good resource endowment and that sort of thing, is whether the particular policy makers can be relied upon to acquire new debt in a responsible manner, and that is very difficult to assess.

But let us come back to the data question. I do not think the World Bank has very much truly confidential data, although we have a minor amount in some special cases. Most of the information that we base our analysis on is, in fact, available to commercial banks. It simply takes a lot of digging out, because the countries that one is talking about often do not publish data in a timely manner. The data are usually available, but one has to go and get it. That is very time-consuming.

What does this mean in practical terms for banks? Perhaps they should reexamine, without necessarily increasing, the economists' time already spent. Thus, they might usefully compare the proportion of economists' time spent analyzing the prospects of various countries to the shares of portfolio and profit attributable to those countries. I make this suggestion because my informal inquiries indicate that the predominant part of economists' time in major U.S. banks is spent on analyzing aspects of the U.S. economy. Although many banks have over 15 percent of their profit originating from developing countries, few devote that high a share of their analytical time to them. And yet, the fact is that the economies where the data is missing and where you need most of the original analysis and the judgment are precisely those of the developing countries and not of the United States.

One wonders how long the commercial banking world will continue to expand their portfolios in the absence of more readily available data. This must be partly a function of the competitive nature of the international lending business. As we move from a borrowers' market to a lenders' market, and as various lenders reach prudent exposure limits on the basis of present knowledge, I would expect to see a growing insistence by commercial banks on obtaining the already available data and on making real improvements in the data base. To facilitate this process, one wonders whether it would not be advantageous for both the international banking community and the major borrowers to come to some form of agreement about what information it is reasonable for banks to ask for. I emphasize this matter of information, data, and analysis because it is my sincere belief that improvements here are in the interests of the developing countries themselves, and are likely to lead to a greater, rather than a lesser, willingness by commercial bankers to take on increased developing-country exposure and to expand the coverage to a wider range of borrowers.

My last comment is that for this type of country analysis one has to look forward and not backward. A similar stance was, I think, taken by Brackenridge. This means, for me personally, having dealt with creditworthiness for some time, that I am very cool to the checklist approach. Of course, as James Thornblade indicates, if it is used as one instrument along with many others, the checklist is a useful discipline to go through. But the early-warning system leaves me very cool indeed, because it is essentially backward-looking.

Roman Senkiw

I will concentrate my comments on the chapter by Alice Mayo. I think we should congratulate our colleagues at Eximbank for their efforts on the early-warning model. It is really a pioneering, and a very difficult, area in which they are dealing. In my opinion, the results that they have demonstrated with their model are very encouraging.

I will focus on three general points. First, consider the question of the dependent variable. Brackenridge mentioned the difficulty of defining things like foreign exposure. Defining the appropriate dependent variable for this kind of model is equally troublesome. Choosing a criterion such as reschedulings appears logical in the first instance. But many of these reschedulings do not take place for economic reasons but for political reasons. There is also a difference between official and commercial debt. The variable chosen for the Eximbank model was reschedulings of official debt, but the problem we are concerned with here also involves commercial debt. There is also the question of timing: When does a country really begin to encounter problems? Although a country may be seeking an official debt rescheduling in mid-1976, our bank may have begun to notice repayment difficulties on that country's commercial debt in early 1975. Therefore, one might well ask what is being predicted when official reschedulings are used as the dependent variable. Shouldn't the dependent variable be defined a bit wider, to include such things as rollovers or forced debt restructurings?

There is also the question of fine-tuning the model. It really is not all that helpful to be told that a country will fail sometime over the next five-year period. Very often the critical time interval is from six months to one year. It makes a great difference to a banker whether he makes a one-year loan or a five-year loan.

There is also the question of country coverage. This model deals exclusively with the developing countries. They, however, may not be the main source of danger from the point of view of stability of international financial arrangements. Certain issues raised today throw a question mark on some industrialized countries as well. As a result, shouldn't the model be comprehensive—covering both industrialized as well as developing economies?

This gets us into the second point I'd like to focus on, the problem of the independent variables. There are certainly many ratios which one could pick. The Royal Bank of Canada first launched its own work in this field in early 1975; over 100 ratios were conceptualized. Eventually, due to data problems, we narrowed down this number to around 26 which we tested intensively. Finally, we ended up with 10 ratios that were usable. Data problems are severe, particularly if one is attempting a wide coverage of countries, because ratios common to all these countries must be constructed. The timeliness of the reporting of this data must also be considered. For instance, it may be desirable to include variables relating to foreign debt. But what is the use of incorporating this into the model if this type of data is perenially obsolete? There is also the question of the ratios' predictive power—a critical point in building this type of model. Then, there is the question of forecasting the ratios in order to stretch out the lead time as far as possible. There are many pitfalls here as well, particularly in an environment where structural changes are taking place.

Finally, I would like to add a word of encouragement. The misclassification error in the Eximbank model was 19 percent, a very good result given the difficult area they are dealing with. As a point of comparison, some of the Royal Bank's work has given similar results. One recent run gave an 18 percent misclassification error; another gave 14 percent, which seems to be the right ballpark for these types of models.

I would also offer the general remark that using checklists, as described by James Thornblade, is only better than using nothing at all. The main problem is that checklists add apples and oranges and it is impossible to interpret the meaning of the final number that is derived. It may be of some value to have the person in charge of a country go through such an exercise, but it isn't useful to derive any overall scores by this method. This is, in fact, why the Royal Bank eliminated the checklist system several years ago.

Mathematical models are better. But before anyone attempts to construct such a model, he should keep in mind that he is embarking upon a very expensive project. Even keeping the amount of model development work to a minimum, as the Royal Bank did, the forging of such an analytical tool and its smooth operation can cost in the $100 thousand range.

Another problem is the use of such a tool within the organization, that is, the commercial bank. Ultimately the data have to be communicated to bankers. Bankers have a strong tendency for ranking things; they love to rank countries. Nevertheless, the Royal Bank's country risk index is only marginally useful for cross-country comparisons and certainly not for straight rankings of countries. Its best use is really as an early warning model device on a country-by-country basis.

Another problem is how to translate a given score that is derived by one of these mathematical models into a dollar limit for a country. This may well be a problem with no satisfactory solution. There are many possible formulas, but we have not yet found a workable and acceptable formula for our bank.

We have heard a lot concerning the dimensions of the broad developing-country debt problem and we have looked at methods of measuring this problem. While country-by-country results are interesting in their own right, it would be even more interesting to know what is happening on the broad front. In using the Eximbank model, for example, has there been a notable deterioration in the status of a wide range of countries over the last two years? What about the closing years of the decade? Are the developing countries improving their status or not? This information would help us to see what lies ahead.

William R. Cline

I am impressed with Bruce Brackenridge's description of the massive undertaking that Morgan Guaranty has made in terms of simply finding out what the bank's exposure is. I am also impressed by his comments, and those of John Holsen, on the overriding importance in the country evaluation placed on the quality of management in each country. However, as Jerome Blask informs us, although there is a lot of qualitative work, the amount of quantitative work, especially within the banks, seems to leave something to be desired. It would seem that whether a country is going to be forced to default or to reschedule is essentially an economic question. It should be subject to analysis by focusing on the key economic variables which determine the likelihood of default.

Turning to James Thornblade's paper, I think that the rankings of individual variables is certainly a step in the right direction. One does have to ask, however, what one learns if there is no basis for attaching a weight to each variable in the rankings. One also has to worry about the interaction of the variables and the fact that misleading information can be conveyed if the rankings are done with the variables independently. I'll give one important example. If one looks at the amortization rate, or the length of the outstanding debt, it is typically assumed that the longer the debt the better. However, for a given DSR, the shorter the debt the better, because shorter maturity combined with a given

DSR means less total outstanding debt; it means that the country will be over the problem sooner. Therefore, it is important to consider the interaction of the variables. My only other comment on the Thornblade chapter concerns the per capita income variable. I think the anlaysis in a number of the other chapters suggests that we ought to have second thoughts about whether economic management is positively correlated with per capita income.

With respect to Eximbank's quantitative work, the model represents a massive effort with apparently very good results. It is certainly a good mouse trap and perhaps a better mouse trap. It uses logit analysis instead of discriminant analysis. That's the right thing to do, because discriminant analysis separates countries into completely opposite boxes. For example, it was originally used in determining whether a skull belonged to one Indian tribe or to another. Logit analysis, on the other hand, considers an economic force that gradually rises to a threshold and then pushes beyond that threshold and causes a discrete change; so logit analysis is better than discriminant analysis.

I do have serious reservations about the exclusion of the debt-service ratio in the Eximbank model. This has been the single most important explanatory variable in past efforts including the Frank and Cline model. (I would similarly raise questions about Thornblade's conclusion that there is a poor correlation of the DSR with creditworthiness.) Perhaps the good results obtained by Alice Mayo are saved by the presence of the debt-to-export ratio, which to some extent serves as a proxy for the DSR.

I think the reasoning for excluding the DSR is not really compelling. The reasoning is that, in the actual year of the rescheduling, the observed debt service is different from what it would have been expected to be without the rescheduling. I think the point is that economic policy makers, at the time that they decided to take on the rescheduling, had no more information available than one has now looking at the data. In other words, they also had to have a forecast of what the new DSR would be and a reasonable forecast of export earnings; so I am not convinced that there is any distortion introduced by using the DSR, and I think that perhaps more has been thrown out than gained on this point.

I think that rather than dealing with some of the other more detailed comments, I would like to take the liberty of answering Roman Senkiw's question with respect to what some of these models say about where we are today. Gordon Smith of Rice University has just completed a study for the Overseas Development Council which applied the Frank and Cline model and the Feder and Just (early-warning) model to 1976-77 forecast data for some 25 developing countries. It turns out that there is no radical deterioration now, as compared with the early 1970s, in the creditworthiness of most developing countries. This is a result that is consistent with Anthony Solomon's comments. I think that one of the key factors here is that inflation has saved the day; it has essentially eroded the real value of dollar debt outstanding so that the large nominal values don't mean much.

These exercises by Smith did indicate a number of important countries that have serious problems. They tend to fall into three clusters. One cluster includes countries which have experienced a collapse in the price of a key export. Here we find Chile, Peru, Zaire, and Zambia, with the copper price collapse as the case in point. Another cluster is of very poor countries with long-term debt problems such as Bangladesh and Pakistan. The other countries include Mexico and also, if private debt is included, Brazil. However, if one looks only at public debt, Brazil does not appear to be in debt difficulty. Now, in this third cluster I think it's clear that the heavy emphasis on economic management enters into the picture. What the standard model predicts is then a background and one looks at the economic management team to see whether a departure from the standard analysis is warranted. The judgment of the financial community in the past and the present has been that such a departure is justified for Brazil and Mexico.

ABOUT THE EDITOR AND CONTRIBUTORS

STEPHEN H. GOODMAN is Director, Foreign Risk Analysis, The Singer Company. From March 1975 to August 1977 he was Vice President, Policy Analysis, the Export-Import Bank.

He received a B.S. in economics from Cornell University, an M.A. in economics from Yale University, and an M.Ph. in economics from Yale University.

Mr. Goodman has taught economics at Yale University and at the University of Zambia. He was an analyst in the Office of Economic Research, Central Intelligence Agency, from 1969 until 1975, directing the Agency's analytical efforts in international trade and finance. A specialist in international finance and the problems of the developing countries, Mr. Goodman is the author of many articles and papers.

ROBERT Z. ALIBER is professor of International Economics and Finance, University of Chicago Business School. He received his Ph.D. in economics from Yale University and has been a member of the Business School faculty since 1967. A specialist in international finance, Professor Aliber is the author of many articles and books.

ANTHONY G. BARRETT is a Financial Economist at the Export-Import Bank. He received his M.A. in economics from Brown University and is currently working toward a Ph.D. in economics at George Washington University.

DAVID O. BEIM is an International Investment Adviser. He received his B.A. in mathematics from Stanford University and spent a year at Oxford University as a Rhodes scholar. He was Executive Vice President in charge of Eximbank's direct credit program until June 1977 and was a Vice President at the First Boston Corporation before joining Eximbank.

JEROME K. BLASK is a Financial Economist at the Export-Import Bank. He received his B.A. in economics from Dickinson College and has taught economics at George Washington University. Mr. Blask is now completing work toward his J.D. at the Georgetown University Law Center.

A. BRUCE BRACKENRIDGE is Senior Vice President and Senior Credit Officer of the International Banking Division of Morgan Guaranty Trust Company. He received his B.A. in Philosophy from Williams College and then joined Morgan Guaranty. Prior to becoming a Senior Vice President, Mr. Brackenridge was President of Morgan Guaranty International Finance Corporation.

WILLIAM R. CLINE is a Senior Fellow at the Brookings Institution. He received his Ph.D. in economics from Yale University. Before joining Brookings in 1973, Mr. Cline was an Assistant Professor at Princeton University and served with the U.S. Treasury Department and the Ford Foundation.

STEPHEN M. DUBRUL, JR. is a business consultant and private banker. From January 1976 until April 1977 he was President and Chairman, Export-Import Bank. He received his M.B.A. from Harvard Business School. Mr. DuBrul was a Senior Managing Director and Director at Lehmann Brothers, Inc., until 1972 and general partner at Lazard Freres Company from 1972 until 1976.

STEPHEN D. ECCLES is Chief, Southern Agricultural Division for Eastern Africa, the World Bank. He received his M.A. in mathematics from Cambridge University and later served with the British Foreign Service and the United Nations Development Program. At the time of the conference, Mr. Eccles was Senior Financial Advisor and Chief of the Bank's Loan Portfolio Analysis.

RICHARD D. ERB is a Resident Scholar at the American Enterprise Institute. He received his Ph.D. in economics from Stanford University. He is a former Assistant Director, Council on International Economic Policy, and Deputy Assistant Secretary for Developing Nations, U.S. Treasury Department.

IRVING S. FRIEDMAN is Senior Vice President and Senior Adviser for International Operations, Citibank. He received his Ph.D. in economics from Columbia University. Mr. Friedman was a Senior Economist and Adviser at the International Monetary Fund and at the World Bank before joining Citibank in 1974.

JOHN A. HOLSEN is Chief Economist, Latin America and Caribbean Region, the World Bank. He received his M.A. in economics from the University of Chicago. Mr. Holsen has served with USAID in Chile and with the U.S. Economic Mission in Spain. He has been with the World Bank since 1966.

CHARLES P. KINDLEBERGER is a Professor Emeritus of economics at MIT. He received his Ph.D. in economics from Columbia University and has been a member of the economics faculty at MIT since 1948. A specialist in international economics and international economic history, Professor Kindleberger is the author of many articles and books.

LAWRENCE B. KRAUSE is a Senior Fellow at the Brookings Institution. He received his Ph.D. in economics from Harvard University. Mr. Krause served on the staff of the Council of Economic Advisers and the economics faculty at Yale University before joining the Brookings Institution in 1963.

ALICE L. MAYO is a Country Economist at the Export-Import Bank. She received her M.A. in economics from Georgetown University in 1972. Before joining the Export-Import Bank in 1976, Ms. Mayo served with the Federal Preparedness Agency and the U.S. Department of Transportation.

JO W. SAXE is Chief, International Finance Division, Economic Analysis and Projections Department, the World Bank. He received his D.Phil. from Oxford. Mr. Saxe joined the World Bank as a consultant in 1968 and has been Chief of the International Finance Division since 1972.

ROMAN SENKIW is a Senior Economist, Royal Bank of Canada. He received his Ph.D. in economics from the University of Virginia. Mr. Senkiw served with the International Monetary Fund and several government agencies in Canada before joining the Royal Bank in 1974.

ROBERT L. SLIGHTON is a Vice President and Senior Economist at the Chase Manhattan Bank. He received his Ph.D. in economics from Johns Hopkins University. He is a former Research Associate at the Rand Corporation, National Intelligence Officer for Economics at the Central Intelligence Agency, and Deputy Assistant Secretary for Research at the Treasury Department.

ANTHONY M. SOLOMON is Undersecretary, U.S. Treasury Department. He received his M.A. in economics and his M.P.A. from Harvard University. Mr. Solomon was a lecturer and member of the faculty at the Harvard Business School from 1961 to 1963. He is a former Deputy Assistant Secretary of State for Latin America and Assistant Secretary of State for Economic Affairs.

JAMES B. THORNBLADE is a Vice President and Economist at the First National Bank of Boston. He received his Ph.D. in economics from MIT. Before joining the First National Bank of Boston in 1972, Mr. Thornblade was an Assistant Professor at Syracuse University.

HENRY C. WALLICH is a Member of the Board of Governors of the Federal Reserve System. He received his Ph.D. in economics from Harvard University and was a member of the economics faculty at Yale University from 1951 to 1974 when he joined the Board of Governors. A specialist in international finance, Mr. Wallich is the author of many articles and books.

COMMERCIAL BANKS AND ECONOMIC DEVELOPMENT:
The Experience of Eastern Africa

Ali Issa Abdi

POLITICAL RISKS IN INTERNATIONAL BUSINESS:
Investment Behavior of Multinational Corporations

Lars H. Thunell

FINANCING URBAN AND RURAL DEVELOPMENT
THROUGH BETTERMENT LEVIES: The Latin American
Experience

Jorge Macon
José Merino Mañon

MONETARY RELATIONS AND WORLD DEVELOPMENT:
Atlantic Institute Studies IV

edited by Fabio Basagni
Pierre Uri

*FOR A NEW POLICY OF INTERNATIONAL DEVELOPMENT

Angelos Angelopoulos

*Available in paperback.